MW01254434

10 Minute Guide to Quicken® 2 for Windows™

Debbie Walkowski

Revised by Joe Kraynak

alpha books

A Division of Prentice Hall Computer Publishing

11711 North College, Carmel, Indiana 46032 USA

©1992 by Alpha Books

International Standard Book Number: 1-56761-028-5
Library of Congress Catalog Card Number: 92-74559

95 94 93 92   8 7 6 5 4 3 2 1

Interpretation of the printing code: the rightmost double-digit number is the year of the book's printing; the rightmost single-digit number is the number of the book's printing. For example, a printing code of 92-1 shows that the first printing of the book occurred in 1992.

Publisher: *Marie Butler-Knight*
Managing Editor: *Elizabeth Keaffaber*
Product Development Manager: *Lisa A. Bucki*
Acquisitions Manager: *Stephen R. Poland*
Development Editor: *Seta Frantz*
Production Editor: *Lisa C. Hoffman*
Copy Editors: *San Dee Phillips, Barry Childs-Helton*
Editorial Assistant: *Hilary J. Adams*
Cover Design: *Dan Armstrong*
Designer: *Amy Peppler-Adams*
Indexer: *Jeanne Clark*
Production Team: *Tim Cox, Mark Enochs, Joelynn Gifford, Tim Groeling, Phil Kitchel, Tom Loveman, Michael J. Nolan, Mary Beth Wakefield*

Special thanks to Hilary J. Adams for ensuring the technical accuracy of this book.

Screen reproductions in this book were created by means of the program Collage Plus from Inner Media, Inc., Hollis, NH.

Printed in the United States of America

Contents

Introduction

Do you ever get to the end of the month, thinking you've done well on your budget, and then find yourself with no money left to spend? Or do you feel as if your small business is doing well financially, but you'd like to have a better handle on your finances? Quicken for Windows is the program to help you get your personal and business finances in order. You probably don't have time to pore over volumes of user information learning how to use the program. You need to:

- Find your way around Quicken for Windows as quickly as possible.

- Identify those Quicken features that are essential for your particular financial needs.

- Find a clear-cut, plain-English guide that helps you learn how to use the program.

Welcome to the *10 Minute Guide to Quicken 2 for Windows*.

What Is the 10 Minute Guide?

The *10 Minute Guide* series is a new approach to learning computer programs. Because you don't have the time (or inclination) to teach yourself the program or, worse yet, sift through detailed information trying to learn the program, the *10 Minute Guide* teaches you the program's essential features in lessons that you can complete in ten minutes or less. And because each lesson is self-contained, you can start and stop whenever you like, learning at your own pace.

Conventions Used in This Book

Each lesson is set up in an easily accessible format. Steps that you must perform are numbered. Pictures of screens are included to show you what to expect. And the following icons are used to mark definitions, warnings, and tips that help you understand what you're doing and tell you how to avoid trouble:

Plain English icons appear wherever a new term is defined.

Panic Button icons appear where new users commonly run into trouble.

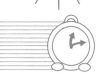

Timesaver Tips offer shortcuts and hints for using the program more effectively.

Version 2 icons point out new features introduced in Quicken 2 for Windows.

In addition, the following conventions are used to provide a clear idea of what to do:

What you type	Information you type appears in bold, color, computer type.
Items you select	Any item you select appears in color. This includes menu and command names, as well as shortcut key combinations. The selection letter for an option appears in bold color.
On-screen text	Any text appearing on-screen is printed in a special computer type.

Using This Book

This book is broken down into a series of lessons. You can read the lessons from beginning to end, or you can skip to the lesson you need right now. The following list provides a guide for using this book.

Learn the Basics   If this is your first encounter with Quicken for Windows and you are not familiar with Windows basics, work through the first three lessons in this book. These lessons provide some basic information about getting around in Quicken for Windows.

Skip Around   You can read the remaining lessons in order, or skip around to the lessons as needed.

Install Quicken 2 for Windows To learn how to install Quicken for Windows, read the instructions on the inside front cover.

Know Quicken's Iconbar The inside back cover shows the icons that appear in the Quicken for Windows iconbar, and what each icon represents.

What Is Quicken for Windows?

Quicken for Windows is a program that helps you manage finances for your home, home office, or small business. With Quicken, you can:

- Keep track of your income and expenses.

- Record transactions for bank and credit card accounts.

- Write and print checks.

- Reconcile bank statements automatically.

- Create monthly budgets.

- Create detailed reports on income and expenses, or generate traditional "accounting" reports such as income statements and balance sheets.

- Keep track of investment accounts.

- Gather information for tax preparation.

You don't have to use all these features. You can pick and choose Quicken features to meet your particular needs.

The nice thing about Quicken for Windows is that it's designed for people who are not accounting or financial wizards. You don't even need to know any accounting terminology to use Quicken.

Acknowledgments

Thanks to the editorial staff at Alpha Books for bringing this book to fruition. Thanks to Seta Franz, for her good-natured critiques; to Lisa Hoffman, for carefully shepherding the book through production; to San Dee Phillips and Barry Childs-Helton, for their careful editing; and to Hilary Adams for making sure the program did what the book said it did.

Thanks also to our unheralded production department at Prentice Hall Computer Publishing for transforming a stack of pages into an attractive, bound book.

Trademarks

All terms mentioned in this book that are known to be trademarks or service marks are listed below. In addition, terms suspected of being trademarks or service marks have been appropriately capitalized. Alpha Books cannot attest to the accuracy of this information. Use of a term in this book should not be regarded as affecting the validity of any trademark or service mark.

Microsoft Windows is a registered trademark of Microsoft Corporation.

Quicken and Quicken for Windows are registered trademarks of Intuit.

Getting Started with Quicken for Windows

In this lesson, you'll learn how to start and exit Quicken, how to select commands from the menus, and how to get help when you need it.

Starting Quicken

You must install Quicken for Windows on your hard disk before you can use it. If you have not yet installed Quicken, turn to the inside front cover of this book and follow the installation instructions. Follow these steps to start the program.

Using the mouse:

1. If necessary, type `cd\windows` at the DOS prompt; then type `win` and press Enter. This starts Microsoft Windows.

2. If the Program Manager window is minimized, move the mouse pointer to the Program Manager icon and press the left mouse button twice quickly.

3. If you cannot see the Quicken program group window, click on Window in the menu bar and click on Quicken.

4. Move the mouse pointer onto the Quicken 2 for Windows icon and press and release the left mouse button twice quickly.

Using the keyboard:

1. If necessary, type `cd\windows` at the DOS prompt; then type `win` and press Enter. This starts Microsoft Windows.

2. If the Program Manager window is minimized, hold down Ctrl and press Esc, press ↓ until `Program Manager` is highlighted, and press Enter.

3. If you cannot see the Quicken program group window, press Ctrl+F6 until the Quicken group is highlighted, and then press Enter.

4. The Quicken for Windows icon is highlighted. Press Enter to start the program.

If you are using Windows 3.1, when you start Quicken for the first time, a message appears asking if you want to learn about Microsoft Windows. Press Alt+Y or click on the Yes button to run the Microsoft Windows tutorial, or press Alt+N or click on the No button to skip the tutorial. If you skip the Windows tutorial, another dialog box appears, asking if you want to view an introduction to Quicken. Take the same steps to proceed with or skip this tutorial.

Setting Up the First Time You Start Quicken

The first time you start Quicken for Windows, the First Time Setup dialog box appears, as Figure 1.1 shows. This dialog box lets you choose home or business categories in Quicken. You will use these categories later to track your income and expenses.

Category choices

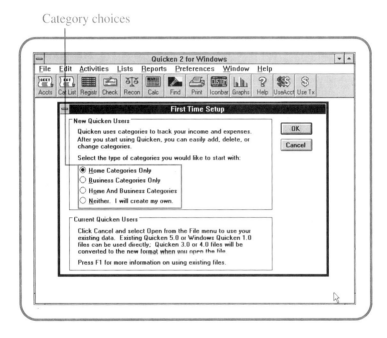

Figure 1.1   The First Time Setup dialog box.

3

Old Quicken Files? If you have account files that you created in a previous version of Quicken (DOS or Windows version), you can use those files instead of creating new ones. Click on the Cancel button in the First Time Setup dialog box, or tab to it and press Enter. Then open the existing account file. For instructions on opening an account file, see Lesson 23, "Working with Quicken Files."

To respond to this dialog box, perform the following steps:

1. Select Home, Business Only, Home and Business, or Neither to specify which set of predefined categories you want to use. (Select an option by clicking on it or by holding down the Alt key while pressing the key that corresponds to the underlined letter in the option's name.)

2. Click on the OK button or tab to it and press Enter. The Select Account Type dialog box appears.

3. Select an account type from the list. (Most users start with a bank account—either checking or savings.)

4. Click on the OK button or tab to it and press Enter. The New Account Information dialog box appears (see Figure 1.2).

5. Type a name for the account in the Account Name text box.

6. Press Tab or click inside the Balance text box, and enter the current balance of the account. (You can get this amount from the most recent bank statement.)

7. Press Tab or click inside the as of text box, and type the date of the current balance.

8. If desired, press Tab or click inside the Description text box, and type a description of the account. For example, type the account number.

9. Click on the OK button or tab to it and press Enter. Quicken creates the account and displays a register for the new account.

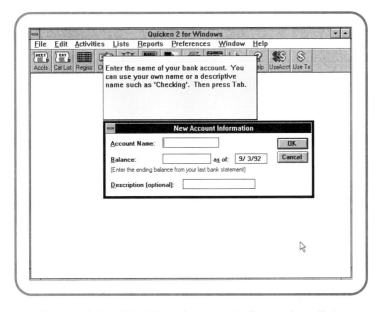

Figure 1.2   The New Account Information dialog box.

The Quicken for Windows Program Window

Now that you have an account, the Quicken for Windows program window appears, as in Figure 1.3. This is the window you'll see whenever you start Quicken.

Control menu box Title bar Menu bar Iconbar   Minimize button Maximize button

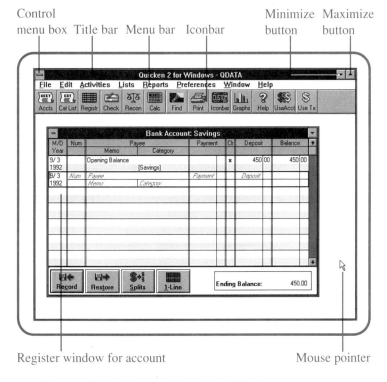

Register window for account   Mouse pointer

Figure 1.3   The Quicken for Windows program window.

Some of the elements that make up the Quicken for Windows program window follow:

Title bar Displays the program name and the title of the account file that's currently open.

Menu bar Lists all menu names. Each menu contains a list of commands. You'll learn to use these in the next lesson.

Iconbar Displays icons (graphical representations) for many of the Quicken commands. You'll learn to use the iconbar in the next lesson.

Minimize button Click on this button to reduce a window to the size of an icon.

Maximize button Click on this button to enlarge the window to full-screen size. If you see a double-headed arrow, this is the restore button; click on it to restore the window to its original size.

Control menu box Displays a pull-down menu that lets you move and resize the window and switch to other Windows programs currently running. Press Alt+Spacebar or click on this box to display the menu.

Getting Help

If you need help performing a task in Quicken, you can use Quicken's on-line help. To get help, pull down the Help menu by clicking on Help in the pull-down menu bar or by pressing Alt+H. Then choose one of the following items from the menu:

Quicken Help   Provides *context-sensitive* help—help
that pertains to the activity you are currently doing. You
can bypass the Help menu and get context-sensitive
help quickly by pressing F1 or clicking on the Help
icon.

How To Use Help   Provides information about how to
use the Help system.

Tutorials   Gives you access to two tutorials: Introduction to Windows (if you have Microsoft Windows 3.1)
and Introduction to Quicken. The Introduction to Windows tutorial leads you through the Windows basics.
The Quicken Concepts tutorial gives you an overall
view of how Quicken works.

Order Supplies   Select this option to print an order
form for ordering checks and other items from Intuit.

About Quicken   Displays the Quicken version number.

When you choose Quicken Help from the Help menu
or press F1, Quicken displays a help window. This window
contains information about how to use a particular Quicken
feature. It also contains two types of *hypertext links* (solid-
and dotted-underlined) that let you get more information about related topics. If you select a topic that is
solid-underlined, Quicken displays a help window for that
topic. If you select a term that is dotted-underlined, Quicken
displays a definition for that term. To select a topic or term,
click on it or tab to it and press Enter.

Navigating the Help System

At the top of the Help window is the following series of buttons designed to help you move around the Help system. To use one of the buttons, click on it or press the key that corresponds to the highlighted letter in the button's name.

Contents   Displays an index of help topics from which you can choose.

Search   Lets you search for a help topic by typing the topic's name or part of its name.

Back   Takes you back to the previous help window.

History   Displays a list of help topics you most recently viewed.

<<   Goes back to a previous help screen in a related series of help screens.

>>   Displays the next help screen in a related series of help screens.

Instant Help with Qcards

Quicken provides help for many of its features and dialog boxes by displaying a Qcard at the top of the dialog box, as Figure 1.4 shows. Most Qcards contain three buttons: one that lets you see the next Qcard, a question mark button that displays a help window for the topic, and a book button that tells you where to look in the Quicken documentation for more information.

Click here to see the next Qcard. Qcard

Click here to see detailed help.

Click here to see a cross-reference to the documentation.

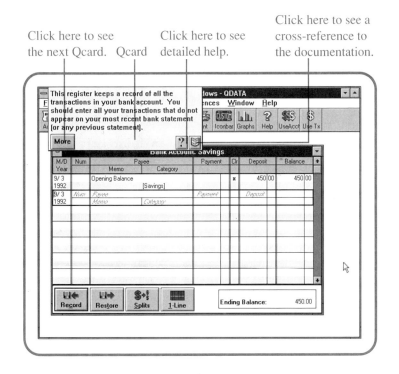

Figure 1.4   Qcards provide immediate help.

Once you are familiar with Quicken, you can turn Qcards off by opening the Preferences menu and choosing Qcards. This displays a dialog box that lets you turn Qcards on or off for various Quicken features.

Exiting Quicken

When you are finished using Quicken, you need to leave the program. Follow these steps:

Using the mouse:

1. Move the mouse pointer onto File in the pull down menu bar and press and release the left mouse button.

2. Move the mouse pointer onto the Exit command, and press and release the left mouse button.

Using the keyboard:

1. Press Alt+F to open the File menu.

2. Press X to select the Exit command.

Quick Exit To exit the program quickly, move the mouse pointer onto the Control menu box (in the upper left corner of the window) and press and release the left mouse button twice quickly.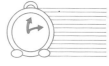

Using Menus and Dialog Boxes

In this lesson, you'll learn how to select Quicken menus and commands, and how to work with the iconbar.

Using the Mouse and the Keyboard

Quicken for Windows is designed to be used with a mouse, although it can be used with the keyboard alone or a combination of the two. This lesson describes how to perform basic functions using both the mouse and the keyboard. In later lessons, we will tell you to *select* an option, and we will leave it up to you to decide whether you want to use the keyboard or mouse.

Table 2.1 lists terms that describe techniques used with the mouse.

Table 2.1   Mouse techniques.

Technique	Operation
Point	Move the tip of the mouse pointer onto the designated item or area of the screen.
Click	Press and release the left mouse button once.
Double-click	Press and release the left mouse button twice quickly.
Drag	Point to an object on-screen and, while holding down the left mouse button, move the mouse.

Selecting Pull-Down Menus and Commands

You can use either the mouse or the keyboard to select commands from the pull-down menus listed on the menu bar.

Commands and Pull-Down Menus   With Quicken for Windows, you issue a *command* to tell Quicken what you want it to do (for example, **P**rint, or **O**pen a file). Commands are listed under the pull-down menus (see Figure 2.1) that appear when you select a menu from the menu bar. They are referred to as pull-down menus because you "pull down" the menu from the menu bar.

Items followed by ellipsis
lead to dialog boxes.   Quick Keys

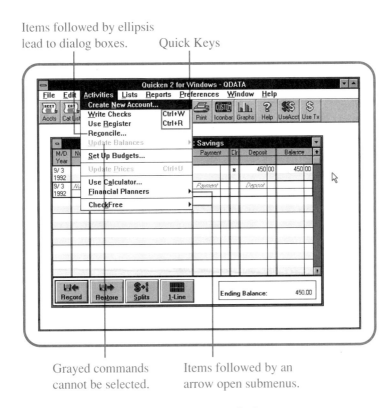

Grayed commands   Items followed by an
cannot be selected.   arrow open submenus.

Figure 2.1   The Activities pull-down menu.

Most commands on the pull-down menus simply issue a command. A command that is followed by an ellipsis (...) displays to a dialog box (explained later in this lesson). A command that is followed by a right-pointing arrow opens to a submenu.

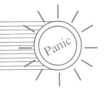

Grayed Commands   When a command doesn't apply to the task you are performing at the time, the command appears grayed on the menu and you cannot select it. For example, the **U**pdate Balances command in Figure 2.1 is grayed because there is no need to update the balance for a new account.

Selecting Commands with the Mouse

To select a menu command using the mouse, follow these steps:

1. Click on the name of the menu in the menu bar. The menu opens to reveal a list of commands.

2. Click on the desired command.

Selecting Commands with the Keyboard

To pull down menus and select commands using the keyboard, you must use the *selection letters* in the menu names and commands. The selection letter is underlined on-screen; in this book, all selection letters are displayed in boldface type. Follow these steps to pull down Quicken menus and enter commands using the keyboard.

1. Press or hold down the Alt key, and press the selection letter in the menu name. The menu drops down to reveal a list of commands.

2. Press the key that corresponds to the selection letter in the command name.

Using Quick Keys in Place of Commands

Many of the commands in Quicken for Windows have corresponding *Quick Keys* that let you bypass the pull-down menus. A Quick Key is usually a two-keystroke combination that represents a Quicken command, such as

Ctrl+O for the **O**pen command to open a file. To help you learn the Quick Keys, Quicken displays the keys on the pull-down menus (see Figure 2.1).

Responding to Dialog Boxes

If you select a menu command that is followed by an ellipsis (...), Quicken displays a dialog box. *Dialog boxes* are separate windows that allow you to provide more specific information about the command you've chosen. They are almost always divided into separate sections and are made up of different elements. Table 2.2 lists dialog box elements and how to use them. Figure 2.2 illustrates some of these elements in the Import From QIF File dialog box that is displayed when you select the Import command from the File menu.

Table 2.2   Dialog box elements.

Element	How To Use It
Text boxes	Type the information requested.
List boxes	Select an item from the list.
Check boxes	When multiple check boxes are displayed, you can select more than one. Each option turns on or off each time you select it.
Drop-down lists	Select an option from the list that drops down when you select the box.
Option buttons	You can choose only one option button when multiple buttons are displayed. Choosing one deselects any other that is selected.
Command buttons	Select the button to execute or to cancel the options you selected.

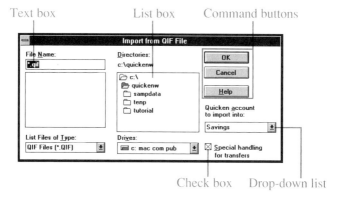

Text box   List box   Command buttons

Check box   Drop-down list

Figure 2.2   Some common dialog box elements.

Using the Mouse in Dialog Boxes

To use the mouse in a dialog box, follow these steps:

1. Click on the dialog box option you want to select. For text boxes, click on the box and type the appropriate text.

2. When all settings are correct, click on OK to close the dialog box.

Using the Keyboard in Dialog Boxes

Use the following techniques to select options or to provide information in a dialog box. When you are told to *select* an option, you can hold down the Alt key and type the selection letter or press Tab. (The Tab key cycles forward through each option in a dialog box. To move backwards, press Shift+Tab.) When an option or setting is selected, it is outlined with a faint dotted line.

Text boxes   Select the text box; then type an entry.

List boxes   Press Alt plus the selection letter in the list box name; use ↑ or ↓ to select an item.

Drop-down lists   Press Tab or Alt+selection letter to select the list (you can press Alt+↓ to display the drop-down list). Use the ↑ and ↓ keys to highlight your choice. Press Tab to accept your selection and move to the next dialog box element.

Option buttons and check boxes   Hold down Alt while typing the selection letter for the option button or the check box you want to select. You can select only one option button in a group. You can select as many check box options as desired.

Command buttons   When there is a selection letter, hold down Alt while pressing the key that corresponds to the selection letter. When there is no selection letter, press Tab until the button is selected (outlined) and press Enter.

Using the Iconbar

The *iconbar* contains a collection of icons that represent menu commands. (Refer to the inside back cover of this book for a list of icons.) Like Quick Keys, icons are designed to make the job of selecting commands quick and easy. To select an icon, just point to it and click. You can select icons only with a mouse; they are not accessible using the keyboard.

Icons   An icon is a picture that represents a program (such as the Quicken icon in the Program Manager window) or a command within a program (such as the Print command used to print a file).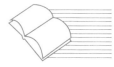

To customize the iconbar, click on the Custom Iconbar icon in the iconbar or pull down the Preferences menu and select Iconbar. The dialog box that appears lets you add, edit, or delete icons from the iconbar or turn off the graphics and/or text portion of the iconbar (to give yourself more room on-screen).

Lesson 3
Using Multiple Quicken Windows

In this lesson, you'll learn about the Quicken windows. You'll learn how to display more than one window at a time, and move, resize, and close windows.

Opening Multiple Windows

As you work with Quicken, you'll find that most of the commands you select from the **Activities**, **Lists**, and **Reports** menus open up separate windows. For example, the Reconcile command on the **Activities** menu opens a window in which you can balance a bank account.

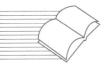

Window A window is a rectangular area that looks like a frame and can be moved or resized. Each window has its own control menu, and maximize and minimize buttons. In Quicken, a window is often the on-screen representation of a familiar item on paper, such as a bank account register.

One of the advantages of using Quicken for Windows is that it opens new windows on-screen without closing those that are already there. So, if the account list is

20

displayed and you select the checking account, the account list remains on-screen and the checking account register appears.

Selecting a Window

With several windows open at the same time, you'll need to move from window to window to enter transactions and perform other tasks. The window in which the cursor is active is known as the *active window*. The title bar of the active window is highlighted and the window is moved to the front, whereas the title bars of other windows are dimmed (see Figure 3.1).

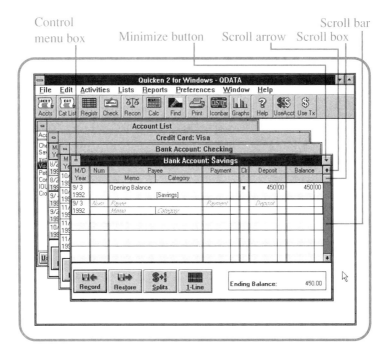

Figure 3.1   Four Quicken windows are cascaded on-screen.

Moving from one window to another with the mouse is easy; just position the mouse pointer anywhere in the new window and click. The window you click on becomes the active window. Using the keyboard, press Ctrl+F6 or Ctrl+Tab until the title bar of the window you want is highlighted. Quicken cycles through the open windows, highlighting the title bar and moving the window to the front as you move from one window to another.

You can also move to a new window by using the **W**indow menu, which lists and numbers all open windows. Pull down the Window menu and type the number of the window or click on its name. The window you choose becomes the active window.

Viewing the Contents of the Active Window

A window often contains more information than can be displayed at once. To maneuver through the contents of a window using the mouse, use the scroll bars (see Figure 3.1):

- To move one line at a time, click on a scroll arrow.

- To scroll continuously, point to a scroll arrow and hold down the left mouse button.

- To move to a position in the window, drag the scroll box up or down inside the scroll bar.

- To move one page up or down, click inside the scroll bar on either side of the scroll box.

Using the keyboard, use the arrow keys to scroll up or down one line at a time, or press the Page Up key to move back or Page Down to move forward a "page" at a time.

Arranging Windows

You can have Quicken arrange the windows for you automatically in a cascade pattern, which "stacks" the open windows, with the active window on top (see Figure 3.1). Follow these steps:

1. Open all the windows you want on-screen at the same time.

2. Pull down the Window menu and select Cascade. Quicken overlaps one window on top of the next as shown in Figure 3.1.

Moving Windows

If you prefer, you can arrange the windows manually by moving each one to a location you choose.

Using the mouse:

1. Move the mouse pointer inside the title bar of the window you want to use, and hold down the left mouse button.

2. Drag the window to a new location and release the mouse button.

Using the keyboard:

1. Press Alt+hyphen to open the Control menu.

2. Select the Move command. A four-headed arrow appears in the title bar of the active window.

3. Use any of the arrow keys to move the window and then press Enter.

Resizing Windows

Resizing windows gives you the flexibility to use screen space in the way most efficient for your particular needs (see Figure 3.2).

To resize windows using the mouse:

1. Move the mouse pointer to any window border until the mouse pointer changes to a double-headed arrow. (If you want to change both the width and height of the window, move the mouse pointer over a corner of the window.)

2. Hold down the mouse button and drag the arrow away from the center of the window to enlarge it, or toward the center of the window to make it smaller.

3. Release the mouse button.

To resize using the keyboard:

1. Press Alt+hyphen to open the Control menu.

2. Select Size. A four-headed arrow appears in the window.

3. Use ↑ and ↓ or ← and → to resize the window.

4. When the window is the desired size, press Enter.

Resized window

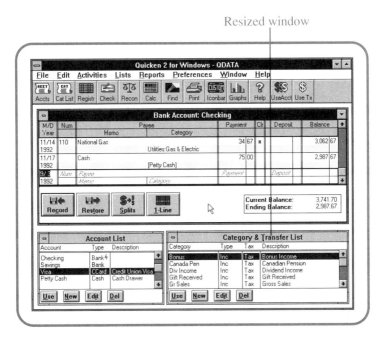

Figure 3.2 Three open windows are resized and rearranged manually.

The Most Screen To maximize Quicken's opening window, click on the maximize button (see Lesson 1, Figure 1.1) in the upper right corner of the window. If you are using a keyboard, press Alt+hyphen to open the Control menu box and select Maximize.

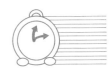

Minimizing Windows to Icons

When you have several Quicken windows open at the same time, you can clear the screen area without actually closing the open windows. This is called reducing, or *minimizing*, a window to an icon. When you minimize a window, an icon appears on-screen in place of the window. Table 3.1 illustrates the icons used for each Quicken account window. (Note that some of these accounts are advanced features of Quicken for Windows and are not discussed in this book.)

Table 3.1   Icons that represent Quicken windows.

Icon	Window
	Bank account
	Credit card account
	Cash account
	Other asset account
	Other liability account
	Investment account

To minimize a window using the mouse, click on the minimize button, as Figure 3.3 shows. Using the keyboard, press Alt+hyphen to open the Control menu and select Minimize.

Minimized windows

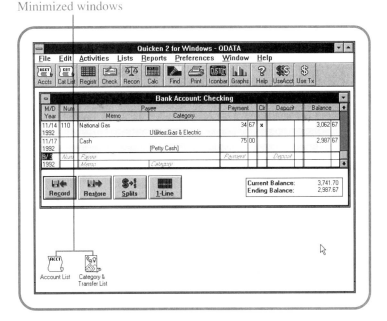

Figure 3.3 One window is open and two windows are minimized.

Restoring Minimized Windows

When you're ready to work again in a window that has been minimized, you restore it. To restore a minimized window using the mouse, double-click on its icon. Using the keyboard, press Ctrl+Tab or Ctrl+F6 to cycle through the window icons. When the icon you want is highlighted, press Alt+hyphen and then select Restore.

Arranging Icons

When you have been doing a lot of moving, rearranging, and minimizing of windows, the window icons can sometimes get lost behind open windows. Quicken provides a command to arrange all window icons so you can see them.

1. Pull down the Window menu.

2. Select Arrange Icons. Quicken arranges all window icons in a row near the bottom of the Quicken window.

Closing Windows

When you are finished using an account, you probably want to close its window to save space on-screen and to conserve computer memory. Here's how.

Using the mouse:

1. Activate the window you want to close.

2. Click on the Control menu box and select Close.

Or:

Double-click on the Control menu box. Quicken closes the active window.

Using the keyboard:

1. Activate the window you want to close.

2. Press Alt+hyphen to open the Control menu.

3. Select Close. Quicken closes the active window.

Lesson 4

Setting Up Accounts

In this lesson, you'll learn how to set up an account and select one when you want to work with it, how to make changes to an account, and how to delete an account you no longer need.

Types of Accounts

An *account* is a record of all financial transactions for an individual item (such as a credit card) and includes a running balance. You can create multiple accounts for each Quicken file. Transactions often affect two or more accounts, such as when you write a check to pay a credit card bill. You'll learn more about transactions in Lesson 7 and Quicken files in Lesson 23.

In Quicken, there are six different types of accounts you can create:

Bank Create a bank account to record checking, savings, or money market transactions.

Credit Card Create a credit card account to record charges, credits, and payments made with a credit card.

Cash   Create a cash account to keep track of cash expenditures. This type of account is most often used by a business to track petty cash.

Asset   Create a separate asset account for each item you own, such as your home, car, or the inventory owned by your business.

Liability   Create a separate liability account for each item for which you owe money, such as your mortgage, car loan, or capital equipment loan.

Investment   Create an investment account to record stock, bond, or mutual fund transactions.

When you create an account, Quicken for Windows automatically creates a *register*, in which all transactions that affect the balance of the account are recorded.

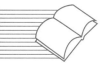

What Is a Transaction?   A transaction is any activity that affects the balance of the account positively or negatively. For example, a charge against or a payment (credit) on a credit card is a transaction.

Setting Up an Account

To set up an account, follow these steps:

1. Pull down the Activities menu and select Create New Account. The Select Account Type dialog box appears, as shown in Figure 4.1.

2. Select the type of account you want to create and then select OK. The New Account Information dialog box appears (see Figure 4.2).

3. Type a name for the account in the Account Name text box.

4. Press Tab or click inside the Balance text box, and enter the current balance of the account. (You can get this amount from the most recent bank statement.)

   If you are setting up an investment account, select the Account contains a single mutual fund check box if applicable. (This check box appears only when you select Investment as the account type.)

5. Press Tab or click inside the as of text box, and type the date of the current balance.

6. If desired, press Tab or click inside the Description text box, and type a description of the account. For example, type the account number.

7. If you are creating a credit account, press Tab or click inside the Credit Limit text box and type the credit limit.

8. Click on the OK button or tab to it and press Enter. Quicken creates the account and a register for the new account appears.

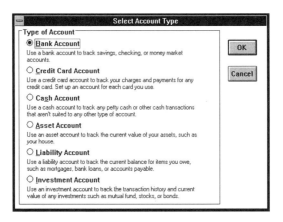

Figure 4.1 The Select Account Type dialog box.

Figure 4.2 The New Account Information dialog box.

Selecting an Account

Before you can enter or review transactions, you must select the account you want to work with (for example, savings or checking). Follow these steps:

1. Pull down the Lists menu and select Account. Quicken for Windows displays the Account List window shown in Figure 4.3.

2. Double-click on the account you want to use, or press ↑ or ↓ to highlight the name and select the Use button or press Enter. The register window for the selected account appears on-screen.

Get to It!   Press Ctrl+A or click on the Accts icon in the iconbar to display the Account List window.

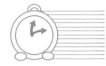

Account List					
Account	Type	Description	Trans	Balance	Chks
Checking	Bank✓		19	2,987.67	✓
Savings	Bank		1	450.00	
Visa	CCard	Credit Union Visa	7	1,067.31	
Petty Cash	Cash	Cash Drawer	3	255.00	
Computer Stuff	Oth A	Computer Equipment	1	4,236.00	
IOU	Oth L		1	345.00	
Crowley's	Invst		0	0.00	

[Use] [New] [Edit] [Del]

Figure 4.3   The Account List window.

Editing an Account

Sometimes you'll need to edit an account; for example, you may need to change the credit limit on a credit card account or change the name or description of an account. Here's how:

1. Pull down the Lists menu and select Account. The Account List window appears (see Figure 4.3).

2. Highlight the account you want to edit and select the Edit button. Quicken displays the Edit Account Information dialog box for the selected account.

3. Change the account name, description, and/or credit limit (if this is a credit account) in the appropriate box and select OK.

Deleting an Account

When you no longer need an account, you should delete it
to keep your file clean and up-to-date.

Deletions Are Forever   Delete an account only if
you are sure you will never need the account or the
records it contains ever again.

To delete an account, perform the following steps:

1. Pull down the Lists menu and select Account.

2. Highlight the account you want to delete and select the
   Del command button. Quicken displays the Deleting
   Account dialog box.

3. To permanently delete the file, type yes and select OK.
   The account is removed from the Account List window.

Lesson 5

Setting Up Categories

In this lesson, you'll learn what categories and subcategories are, how to set them up, and how to print the Category List.

Using Categories and Subcategories

By using categories in Quicken, you can identify where your money is coming from or going to. For example, you can use separate categories to keep track of interest income, salary, and bonus income. If you decide to create a budget, you can use categories to keep track of various expenses, such as auto expenses, groceries, and entertainment. When you create a report or graph, Quicken breaks down your income and expenses into the assigned categories, giving you a clear picture of where your money is flowing.

Quicken provides some predefined categories and subcategories—approximately 40 for home finance and 17 for business use. You can delete, add to, or modify any of the standard categories Quicken provides, or you can create your own. The first time you start Quicken, you set up the program to use home, business, or both types of categories. The Category & Transfer List window (shown in Figure 5.1) lists all existing categories for the active Quicken file.

To display this list, pull down the Lists menu and select Category & Transfer, or press Ctrl+C, or click on the Cat List icon in the iconbar.

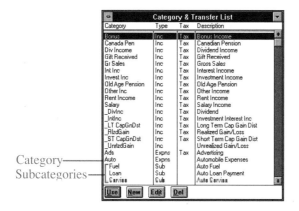

Figure 5.1   The Category & Transfer List window.

Creating Categories and Subcategories

To create a new category or subcategory, follow these steps:

1. Pull down the Lists menu and select Category & Transfer. Quicken displays the Category & Transfer List window shown in Figure 5.1.

2. Select the New button. Quicken displays the Set Up Category dialog box (see Figure 5.2).

3. Type a category name in the Name text box (for example, Landscaping).

4. Type a description for the category in the Description text box.

5. Select Income or Expense for the type of category.

   Or:

   If you are creating a subcategory, select Subcategory of, open the drop-down list, and select the name of the category under which you want this new subcategory listed.

6. Select OK. Quicken adds the new category to the Category & Transfer List window.

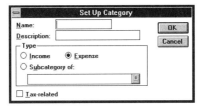

Figure 5.2   The Set Up Category dialog box.

Printing the Category List   Print the category list and keep it near your computer for use as a quick reference. To print the list, first open the category list and then press Ctrl+P or click on the Print icon in the iconbar. Then, select Printer and select the Print button.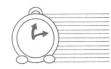

Editing Categories

When you want to make changes to a category name, type, or description, you can edit the category by following these steps:

1. Pull down the Lists menu and select Category & Transfer.

2. Highlight the category you want to edit.

3. Select the Edit button. Quicken displays the Edit Category dialog box.

4. Type a new category name in the Name text box, if desired.

5. Type a new description for the category in the Description text box, if desired.

6. Select Income or Expense for the type of category.

   Or:

   If the category is to be a subcategory, select Subcategory of, open the drop-down list, and select the name of the category under which you want this subcategory listed.

7. When all changes are correct, select OK.

   If you changed a category name, Quicken updates all applicable transactions in account registers to reflect the new name.

Tax Categories

Quicken lets you specify categories as tax-related. For example, if you keep track of day-care expenses for your children, you should mark the Childcare category as tax-related. Then, before you complete your income tax return, you can have Quicken generate a tax report that shows the total childcare expenses and any other tax-related expenses you incurred for the year.

You can designate a new category as tax-related when you create it, or you can edit a category to make it tax-related. Here's how:

1. Pull down the Lists menu and select Category & Transfer.

2. Select the New button or highlight an existing category and select the Edit button. Quicken displays the Set Up Category or the Edit Category dialog box. If creating a new category, follow the steps outlined previously for creating a new category.

3. Select the Tax-related check box and select OK. Quicken marks the category as tax-related in the Category & Transfer List window.

Deleting Categories

Given all the categories Quicken provides, there may be some that you won't need. There's no need to keep these categories in your file if you aren't going to use them.

Delete Cautiously When you delete a category, Quicken automatically deletes the category reference from all transactions to which the category was applied. Be absolutely certain you want to do this before proceeding.

To delete a category, perform the following steps:

1. Pull down the Lists menu and select Category & Transfer.

2. Highlight the category you want to delete.

3. Select the Del button. Quicken displays a warning reminding you that you are about to permanently delete a category.

4. If you're sure you want to delete the category, select Delete.

Setting Up Classes

In this lesson, you'll learn what classes are and how to create them.

Using Classes and Subclasses

Categories help you manage individual income and expense transactions, but they don't tell you where, to whom, or to what each transaction applies. To answer these questions, you apply a *class* to a transaction. For example, suppose you use Quicken to manage your consulting business, and you want to break down your income and expense transactions by client. You can apply a class to each transaction to identify each client. Here are some other examples of how you might use classes:

- If you use Quicken to manage a construction business, you can use classes to identify individual construction jobs.

- If you use Quicken to manage both personal and business finances, you can use two classes—home and business—to keep your transactions separate.

- If you use Quicken to manage a retail business with two outlets, you can use classes to identify transactions for each location.

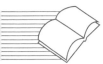 **What Is a Class?**   A class is a label you can apply to a transaction that tells you where, to whom, or to what the transaction applies.

You can display a list of all classes by pulling down the Lists menu and selecting Class or by pressing Ctrl+L. The Class List window is shown in Figure 6.1.

Figure 6.1   The Class List window.

Creating Classes

To create a class, follow these steps:

1. Pull down the Lists menu and select Class. Quicken displays the Class List window.

2. Select the New button at the bottom of the window. Quicken displays the Set Up Class dialog box (see Figure 6.2).

3. In the Name box, type a name for the class.

4. In the Description box, type a description for the class and select OK. Quicken adds the new name to the Class List.

Figure 6.2 The Set Up Class dialog box.

Editing Classes

When you want to change the name or description of a class, you edit the class. Here's how:

1. Pull down the Lists menu and select Class. Quicken displays the Class List window.

2. Highlight the name of the class you want to edit.

3. Select the Edit button at the bottom of the window. Quicken displays the Edit Class dialog box.

4. Type a new name in the Name box, if desired.

5. Type a new description in the Description box, if desired, and select OK. Quicken displays the new name and description in the Class List.

When you change a class name, Quicken automatically updates all applicable transactions in the account registers to reflect the new name.

Deleting Classes

When you no longer want to use a class, you can delete it from the class list by following the steps below.

Delete Cautiously   When you delete a class name, Quicken automatically deletes the name from all transactions to which the class was applied. Be absolutely certain you want to do this before proceeding.

1. Pull down the Lists menu and select Class.

2. Highlight the name of the class you want to delete.

3. Select the Del button. Quicken warns you that you are about to permanently delete a class name.

4. Select OK to delete the selected class. Quicken deletes the name from the Class List window.

Creating Subclasses

Just as categories can have subcategories, classes can have subclasses. A subclass is a label that lets you further refine the classifications you apply to transactions. For example, if you create classes to identify each of your clients, you might create subclasses to identify the individual projects or jobs for each client.

In the Class List window, subclasses are not distinguished from classes. The only place they are distinguished is in the register where you enter transactions. You'll learn about assigning classes and subclasses to transactions in Lesson 7. The procedures for creating, editing, and deleting subclasses are identical to those for classes. Use the steps given for classes to perform those operations for subclasses.

Lesson 7

Entering Transactions

In this lesson, you'll learn how to enter transactions in a register and assign categories and classes to transactions.

Opening the Register

In Lesson 4 you learned how to set up accounts. Each account you set up has a *register*. For example, when you create a checking account, Quicken creates a register similar to the paper check register you use to record the checks you write and the deposits you make.

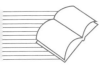

What Is a Register?   A register is a record of all transactions—positive or negative—that affect the balance of an account. Quicken automatically creates a register for each account you create.

This lesson describes how to use the check register (see Figure 7.1). Once you learn how to use the check register, you'll be prepared to use other kinds of Quicken registers (such as the registers for credit card or cash accounts). Other registers are discussed in Lessons 15, 16, and 17.

To display a register, perform the following steps:

1. Pull down the Lists menu and select Account.

2. Highlight the account whose register you want to use, and select the Use button or press Enter.

Transactions   Payee   Cleared transaction   New balance

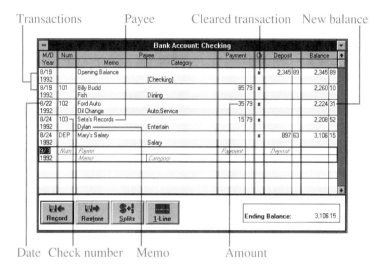

Date   Check number   Memo   Amount

Figure 7.1   The Quicken check register.

Setting Transaction Preferences

Before you begin entering transactions, you might want to choose some of the settings that affect the way the Quicken register works. When you pull down the Preferences menu and select General, Quicken displays the General Settings dialog box (see Figure 7.2). Change any of the following settings and then select the OK button.

47

- **R**equest Confirmation   Use this setting if you want Quicken to request confirmation when you change an entry in a register.

- Color Shading in Register   Use this setting if you want Quicken to use colors (or shading) to distinguish the transaction amount from the balance.

- Enter Key Moves Between Fields in Register and Write Checks   Use this setting to use the Enter key rather than the Tab key to move from one field to the next.

- **B**eep when Recording and Memorizing   Select this option to turn off the beep that sounds whenever you record or memorize a transaction

- **W**arn Before Recording Uncategorized Transactions   If you want Quicken to require you to enter a category, check this box.

- Use **T**ax Schedules with Categories   If you use tax-preparation software to prepare your taxes, check this box to transfer tax-related information from Quicken reports to your tax-preparation software. This is an advanced feature that is not covered in this book. See the Quicken User Manual for more information or refer to the user manual for your tax-preparation software.

- Date Style   Quicken offers two date styles: **MM/DD/YY**, and **DD/MM/YY**.

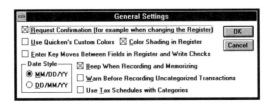

Figure 7.2   The General Settings dialog box.

Moving Around the Register

Using the mouse, you can move anywhere in the register by just pointing and clicking. You can also point and click to move to a specific field in a transaction. If you are using the keyboard, use the keys or keystrokes listed in Table 7.1 to move around the register.

Table 7.1 Keys used for moving around the register.

Keystroke:	Action:
Tab	Moves forward one field.
Shift+Tab	Moves back one field.
↑	Moves back one transaction at a time.
↓	Moves forward one transaction at a time.
Page Up	Scrolls back one screen at a time.
Page Down	Scrolls forward one screen at a time.
Ctrl+Home	Moves to the first transaction in the register.
Ctrl+End	Moves to the last transaction in the register.
Ctrl+Page Up	Moves to the first transaction in the current month.
Ctrl+Page Down	Moves to the first transaction in the next month.

Entering Transactions

Follow these steps to enter transactions in the check register. Use Tab to move between fields. Or, if you have modified your preferences as described earlier in this lesson, use Enter.

49

Drop-Down Lists in the Register Some fields in the register contain drop-down lists. When you tab to or click in the field, the list drops down. Either select an entry from the list or type in an entry. See Lesson 10 for more details.

1. To change the date, move the cursor to the M/D Year field of the first blank transaction line, and type the date in the form MM/DD or DD/MM (depending on your setup selection).

2. If the transaction is for a check, move to the Num field and type the check number. If the transaction is not for a check, you can leave the field blank or type or select a code to help you identify the transaction (for example, ATM for Automatic Teller Machine).

3. Move to the Payee field and type the name of the person or company to which the check is made out or type a description of the deposit or withdrawal.

4. If the transaction is a withdrawal (or payment), move to the Payment field and type the amount.

   Or:

   If the transaction is for a deposit to the account, move to the Deposit field and enter the amount.

5. To enter additional information about the transaction, move to the Memo field, and type an entry.

6. To assign categories or classes to the transaction before saving it, skip ahead to the next section.

7. To save the transaction, press Enter or select the Record command button. Quicken automatically calculates the current balance and moves the cursor to the next blank transaction line.

Assigning Categories and Classes to Transactions

The previous steps outline how to enter transactions without assigning categories or classes. Remember, you aren't required to use categories or classes with Quicken. If you choose to use categories and classes, follow these steps:

1. Complete the transaction as explained in the previous section.

2. Move to the Category field, and select a category from the drop-down list in the register, press Ctrl+C, or click on the Cat List icon in the iconbar. The Category & Transfer List appears (see Figure 7.3).

3. Highlight a category or subcategory in the list and press Enter or select the Use button. Quicken automatically enters the category name in the Category field in the register.

4. To enter a class, move the cursor to the end of the category/subcategory name, and type a slash (/).

5. Press Ctrl+L or pull down the Lists menu and select Class.

6. Highlight a class or subclass in the list and press Enter or select the Use button. Quicken automatically enters the class name in the Category field following the category name.

7. To save the transaction, press Enter or select the Record button.

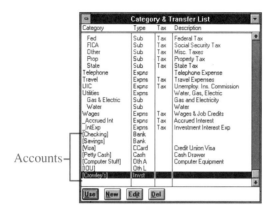

Figure 7.3 The Category & Transfer List dialog box.

Quicken uses a colon (:) to separate categories from subcategories and classes from subclasses. Quicken uses a slash (/) to separate classes from categories. For example, if you chose the Utilities category, the Water subcategory, the Construction class, and the Larson subclass, the notation in the Category field would read: Utilities:Water/Construction:Larson.

Creating New Categories In Lesson 5, you learned how to set up categories using the **C**ategory & Transfer command on the **L**ists menu. You can also create new categories as you enter new transactions. Just type the category name in the category field. When Quicken can't find the category name in the Category & Transfer List, it automatically adds the new category to the list.

Transferring Funds Between Accounts

Many transactions consist of transferring money from one account to another; for example, you may transfer money from your savings account to your checking account to cover a check. To perform such a transfer, follow these steps:

1. Enter the transaction as explained earlier. You can enter the transaction in either account, but make sure you enter the amount in the correct field (Payment or Deposit), so the money is taken from the source account and deposited in the destination account.

2. In the Category field, type the name of the other account, or display the Category & Transfer List and select the account. (All accounts are listed at the end of the Category & Transfer List and are displayed in brackets, for example [Checking].)

3. Select the Record button. Quicken records the transaction in both accounts, subtracting the amount from the source account and adding it to the destination account.

Lesson 8

Editing Transactions

In this lesson, you'll learn how to search for and make changes to existing transactions and to delete transactions.

Finding Transactions

When you want to edit a transaction, you need a quick way to find the right transaction in the register. For example, if you want to change the dollar amount for a check you wrote to American Rentals, you can find the transaction by searching for that name. You can search for text in any field, including those that contain numbers. Here's how:

1. Pull down the Edit menu and select Find, or press Ctrl+F. Quicken displays the Find window (see Figure 8.1).

2. In the Find text box, type the text you want to search for. The text can be letters or numbers.

3. Select Next to search forward through the register or Previous to search backward. Quicken outlines (or highlights) the first transaction that contains the text

you typed (or tells you that it can't find a match). If this
is the transaction you want, skip to step 6.

4. To go to the next or a previous occurrence of a matching
   entry, select the Next or Previous button.

5. To find other text, move to the Find text box, type a new
   entry, and repeat steps 3 and 4.

6. When you are finished searching, close the Find window by double-clicking on its Control menu box or
   pressing Ctrl+F4.

Enter the text to search for.

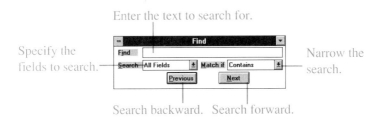

Specify the
fields to search.

Narrow the
search.

Search backward.   Search forward.

Figure 8.1   The Find window.

Narrowing the Search

In the previous section, you searched for all transactions
that contained the specified text. To speed up the search,
you can tell Quicken to search only specific fields. To
narrow the search in this way, pull down the Search drop-
down list in the Find window, and select the field you want
to search.

You can also narrow a search by selecting an option
from the Match if drop-down list. For example, if you want
to find all transactions that are over $1,000, pull down the

Match if drop-down list and select Greater. The complete list of match options follows:

- **Contains** This is the default entry. It finds any entry that contains the specified text.

- **Exact** Finds only those entries that match the Find text exactly.

- **Starts With** Finds only those entries that begin with the Find text.

- **Ends With** Finds only those entries that end with the Find text.

- **Greater** Finds an amount that is greater than the Find text you type.

- **Greater or Equal** Finds an amount that is greater than or equal to the Find text you type.

- **Less** Finds an amount that is less than the Find text you type.

- **Less or Equal** Finds an amount that is less than or equal to the Find text you type.

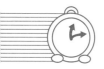

Wild Card Searches When you're not sure exactly what text you're looking for, you can use wild cards to search for unknown characters. For example, if you enter `2**.**` in the Find text box, Quicken finds any numeric entry in the hundreds that begins with 2, such as 250.00 or 232.89. Enter `*sales*` and Quicken finds entries such as Sales Consultants and Equipment Sales in the Description field or Sales in the Category field.

Moving to a Specific Date

If you are using a mouse, you can use the scroll bar to find a transaction on a specific date. When you click on the scroll box and hold down the mouse button, Quicken displays the date of the current transaction in a pop-up box near the Balance column (see Figure 8.2). Drag the scroll box up or down to find the date for which you're looking and release the mouse button. Quicken moves to and outlines (or highlights) the first transaction with a matching date.

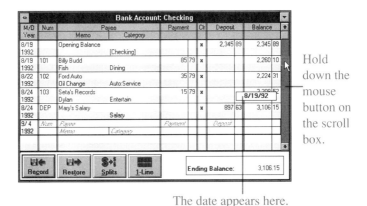

Hold down the mouse button on the scroll box.

The date appears here.

Figure 8.2   The date pop-up box.

Postdated transactions   You cannot use this technique to go to transactions that have a date entry after the current date.

Editing Transactions

Editing transactions includes changing an entry, voiding a transaction, or deleting a transaction. Remember that you can use the Find operation you learned earlier in this lesson to go directly to the transaction you want to edit.

Changing a Transaction

To change a transaction, follow these steps:

1. Select the transaction you want to change. Quicken highlights the transaction.

2. Move to the field you want to change. Quicken selects the entry in the field.

3. Retype the correct entry. Quicken automatically deletes the previous entry, and displays the new entry you type.

4. Select the Record button to change the transaction. If you want to cancel the changes, select Restore before you select Record.

Voiding a Transaction

In order to keep accurate records, it's often better to void a transaction than to delete it. For example, if you make an error writing a check, you probably want to void the transaction (rather than delete it) so you have a record of the check number. Here's how:

1. Select the transaction you want to void.

2. Pull down the Edit menu and select Void Transaction, or press Ctrl+V.

3. Select the Record button. If you want to cancel the void, select Restore before you select Record.

Deleting a Transaction

There are times when it's appropriate to delete a transaction rather than void it. For example, if you enter a transaction in the wrong account register, there is no reason to keep a record of it. When you select Delete Transaction and confirm the deletion, the transaction is permanently deleted and cannot be restored. Be sure you want to delete the transaction before following these steps:

1. Select the transaction you want to delete.

2. Pull down the Edit menu and select Delete Transaction or press Ctrl+D. Quicken displays a message asking you to confirm the deletion.

3. Select Yes to delete the transaction or No to cancel the deletion. When you select **Yes**, Quicken removes the transaction from the register and recalculates the register balance.

Lesson 9

Splitting Transactions

In this lesson, you'll learn how to assign different categories to portions of a transaction.

Using the Splits Window

Sometimes when you enter a transaction in the register, it should apply to *more than one* category, rather than just one. For example, suppose you go to a department store and purchase a car battery and some clothes. If you are keeping track of a budget, you would want to apply the proper dollar amounts to the Auto and Clothes categories, but you don't want to write two separate checks. For these situations, Quicken for Windows allows you to *split* a transaction. You can split a single transaction into as many as 30 categories.

A Split Transaction A split transaction is one in which the total dollar amount shown in the Payment or Deposit field of the register is divided and applied to two or more categories.

To split a transaction as you enter it, follow these steps:

60

1. In the register, enter the transaction date, payee, payment or deposit, and memo (optional), and move the cursor to the Category field.

2. Select the Splits button. Quicken opens the Split Transaction window (see Figure 9.1).

3. Enter a category in the Category field, or press Ctrl+C to display the Category & Transfer List and select a category.

4. (Optional) Move to the Memo field and type a description of the transaction.

5. Move to the Amount field and enter the amount to be applied to the category. Quicken automatically subtracts the amount you enter from the total amount shown in the register, and displays the remainder in the Amount field on the next line.

6. Repeat steps 3–5 for each category you want to use, then select OK. Quicken returns to the register and displays the entry −Splits− in the Category field.

Whenever you want to view the categories for a split transaction, select the transaction and then select the Splits button. Select OK when you're ready to return to the register.

Figure 9.1 The Split Transaction window.

61

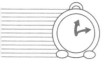 **Using the Split Transaction Window to Add Numbers** You can also use the Split Transaction window to add numbers as you enter them. When you enter a new transaction, leave the Payment or Deposit field blank and select the Splits button. As you enter categories and amounts in the Split Transaction window, Quicken automatically adds the amounts you enter. When you select OK to return to the register, the total amount is shown in the Payment or Deposit field of the transaction.

Editing and Recalculating Split Transactions

You may want to change, or edit, a split transaction once it has been entered. You can change any entry in the Category, Memo, and Amount fields. When you change an entry in the Amount field, the dollar amount must be recalculated. Follow these steps to edit a split transaction.

 **Make Sure the Totals Match** If you've already written a check for the total amount and you edit and recalculate the total splits, make sure the new total matches the check total. Otherwise, your records won't match your bank's records.

1. In the register, select the transaction you want to edit.

2. Select the Splits button to open the Split Transaction window.

3. Select the field you want to edit. Quicken highlights the existing entry.

4. Retype the entry.

5. Repeat steps 3 and 4 for each entry you want to change.

6. If you changed the dollar amount for any entries, select the Recalc button. Quicken automatically recalculates the total amount.

7. Select OK to close the Split Transaction window and return to the register. The recalculated amount is shown in the Payment or Deposit field in the register.

Deleting a Line in a Split Transaction

Rather than changing an entry, you might sometimes want to delete an entire line from a split transaction. For example, say you paid for the battery and the clothes with cash, and you return the battery to the store. You could delete the Auto entry by following these steps:

1. In the register, select the transaction you want to change.

2. Select the Splits button to open the Split Transaction window.

3. Select any field in the line you want to delete.

4. Pull down the Edit menu and select Delete Line Item, or press Ctrl+D. Quicken deletes the entire line.

5. Select the Recalc button to recalculate the transaction total and select OK.

Lesson 10

Working with Memorized Transactions

In this lesson, you'll learn how to memorize recurring transactions, recall and edit memorized transactions, and print a list of all memorized transactions.

What is a Memorized Transaction?

Quicken provides several features to automate the process of entering transactions. Together, these features are called *QuickFill*. With QuickFill, you can have Quicken *memorize* an entire transaction or selected entries. Once you've memorized some transactions, you can *recall* the memorized transactions or portions of the transactions. Using memorized transactions saves you the time of retyping the entries for recurring transactions (such as a mortgage or loan payment) and reduces the chances of errors when entering new transactions.

Quicken stores all memorized transactions in the Memorized Transaction List, from which you can later recall a transaction. The Memorized Transaction List can normally hold up to 3,000 entries. When the list is half full, Quicken displays a message saying that the automatic memorization feature (described in the next section) will be turned off. From that point you can selectively memorize transactions.

Changing the QuickFill Settings

By default, all the QuickFill settings are turned on. After memorizing most of your recurring transactions and after getting accustomed to using Quicken, you may want to turn some of the features off. Table 10.1 provides a list of the QuickFill features. To turn a QuickFill feature on or off, perform the following steps:

1. Pull down the Preferences menu and select QuickFill. The QuickFill Preferences dialog box appears, displaying the options listed in Table 10.1.

2. Select the feature and turn it on or off (an X indicates the feature is on).

3. Select the OK button.

Table 10.1   QuickFill features.

Feature Name	Function
Automatic Memorization of New Transactions	Automatically memorizes each new transaction.
Automatic Completion as You Type an Entry	Completes the entry as you type. For example, if you move to the Category field and type A, Quicken inserts the first category name that starts with A—Auto.
Automatic Recall When Tabbing Out of Payee Field	Recalls all information in the transaction when you press Tab to move from the Payee field to the next field.

continues

Table 10.1 Continued.

Feature Name	Function
Drop Down Lists Automatically	Displays a drop-down list for the active field. When you press Tab to move to a field, the list is automatically pulled down.
Buttons on Quickfill Fields	Instead of displaying a drop-down list in the active field, this option displays only a button. You can click on the button or press Alt+↓ to display the list.

Manually Memorizing a Transaction

If you use Quicken's automatic memorization feature, every transaction you enter is automatically memorized. If you have turned off this feature, follow these steps when you are ready to memorize a new transaction:

1. Enter the new transaction using the steps you learned in Lesson 7. To memorize only a portion of the transaction, type entries in only those fields you want to memorize.

2. Pull down the Edit menu and select Memorize Transaction, or press Ctrl+M. Quicken displays a dialog box saying the transaction is about to be memorized.

3. Select OK to memorize the transaction. Quicken memorizes all entries except the date and the check number.

Memorizing Existing Transactions   You can memorize a transaction after you have entered it by highlighting the transaction and selecting Memorize Transaction from the Edit menu, or by pressing Ctrl+M. Note that when you use this method, Quicken memorizes the entire transaction; you can't choose selected fields to memorize.

Recalling a Memorized Transaction

You can recall an entire memorized transaction or only selected fields in the transaction, depending on the QuickFill settings and on how you like to work. The following sections describe the various techniques for recalling transactions.

Recalling an Entire Transaction

When you are ready to recall an entire memorized transaction, follow these steps:

1. Move to the end of the register, or press Ctrl+N to create a new transaction. (If you don't start with a blank transaction, Quicken overwrites the currently highlighted transaction.)

2. Pull down the Lists menu and select Memorized Transaction, or press Ctrl+T. Quicken displays the list in
alphabetical order by the description field (see Figure 10.1).

3. Select the transaction you want to recall:

   Using the mouse, double-click on the transaction. Use
   the scroll bar, if necessary, to find the correct transaction.

   Using the keyboard, type the first letter of the payee to
   move to that point in the list. If more than one transaction begins with the letter you type, press the letter again
   until the transaction you want is highlighted, and press
   Enter or select the Use button.

4. Make any necessary changes to the transaction entries
   in each field.

5. Select the Record button.

Figure 10.1   The Memorized Transaction List
window.

Recalling a Memorized Transaction Using the Keyboard   You can recall a transaction quickly by typing the first few letters (enough to uniquely identify the payee's name) of the entry in the description field of the register and pressing Tab. Quicken finds the entry that matches the characters you type. If more than one entry begins with the letters you type, Quicken goes to the first entry. Keep typing until the desired entry appears.

Automatically Completing Field Entries

If you have the Automatic Completion setting turned on, Quicken automatically inserts an entry into the current field as you type (see Figure 10.2). For example, if you start typing a name in the Payee field, Quicken inserts the first payee name that appears in its list of memorized transactions. If the name is farther down the list, keep typing until Quicken inserts the desired name. You can use this feature to quickly insert the names of payees, categories, classes, and transfer accounts.

Selecting Entries from Drop-Down Lists

For various transaction fields, Quicken can display drop-down lists that let you select memorized field entries. If the Drop Down Lists Automatically option is turned on, the list drops down as soon as you tab to the field. If the Buttons on QuickFill Fields option is turned on, a drop-down list button appears to the right of the active field, as Figure 10.3 shows. Click on the button or press Alt+↓ to display the list.

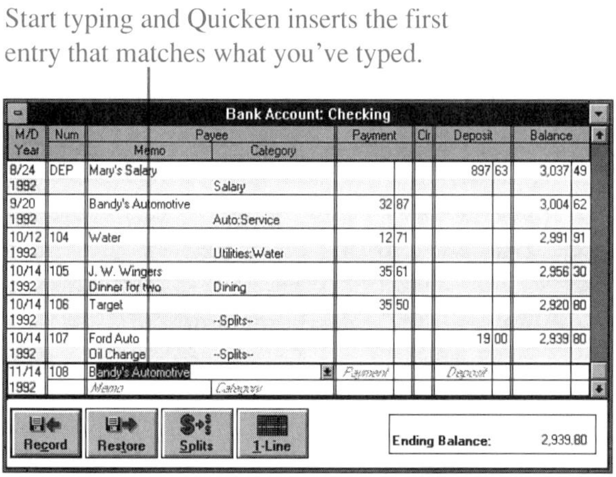

Start typing and Quicken inserts the first
entry that matches what you've typed.

Figure 10.2   With Automatic Completion, Quicken
inserts the first entry that matches what you type.

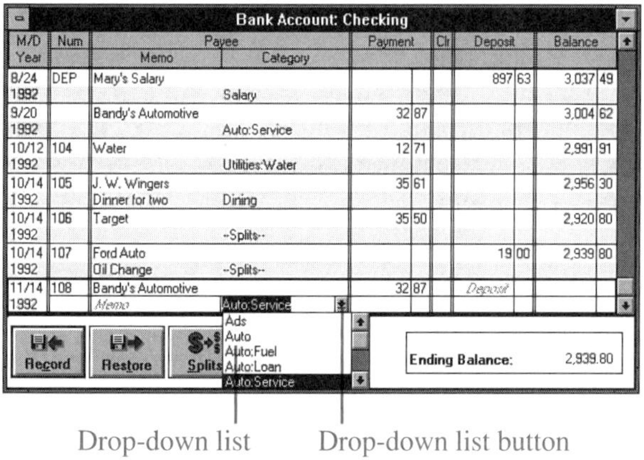

Drop-down list   Drop-down list button

Figure 10.3   With drop-down lists, you can select
an entry rather than typing it.

Editing a Memorized Transaction

You can edit a memorized transaction at any time by performing the following steps:

1. Pull down the Lists menu and select Memorized Transaction, or press Ctrl+T.

2. Highlight the transaction you want to change, and select the Edit button. The Edit Memorized Transaction dialog box appears (see Figure 10.4).

3. Enter your changes, and then select the OK button.

Figure 10.4 The Edit Memorized Transaction dialog box.

Keep Track of Interest and Principal If you have a mortgage, you know that with each mortgage payment, you pay less on interest and more toward the principal of the loan. If you want to keep track of total interest payments on your mortgage (for tax purposes), select the Amortize button in the Edit Memorized Transaction dialog box. Enter the requested information, and Quicken will keep track of the amount of money that goes toward principal and interest with each payment.

Deleting a Memorized Transaction

You can delete a memorized transaction from the list at any time. When you delete a transaction, Quicken permanently removes it from the Memorized Transaction List. Here's how:

1. Press Ctrl+T, or pull down the Lists menu and select Memorized Transaction.

2. Highlight the transaction you want to delete, and select the Del button. Quicken displays a warning saying you are about to delete the transaction.

3. Select OK to delete the transaction or Cancel to save the transaction.

Lesson 11

Creating Transaction Groups

In this lesson, you'll learn how to group transactions to save you time, and you'll learn how to use Quicken's reminder features to help you remember when to pay bills.

Setting Up a Transaction Group

A *transaction group* is a set of transactions that are entered into a register at about the same time. It can include weekly payroll checks or a group of bills that are due at the beginning of the month.

To set up a transaction group, you name the group first and add memorized transactions to it. (**Note:** Before you can create a transaction group, you must have already memorized the transactions you want to include.) Perform the following steps to create a transaction group.

1. Pull down the Lists menu and select Transaction Group, or press Ctrl+J.

2. Select one of the transaction groups labeled <unused>, and select the Edit button. Quicken displays the Describe Group window (see Figure 11.1).

3. In the Name for this group text box, enter a name (up to 20 characters) that describes the group of transactions. For example, if the group includes bills paid at the end of the month, you might name the group End-of-Month Bills.

4. For all types of accounts other than Investment, select the Regular option under Type of transactions.

5. If you want to use Quicken's reminder features (discussed later in this lesson), select an option from the Frequency drop-down list and enter the date the transactions are due next in the Next scheduled date box.

6. When all settings are correct, select OK. Quicken displays the Assign Transactions to Group window, showing a list of all memorized transactions (see Figure 11.2).

7. Select the memorized transactions you want to add to the group:

   • Using the mouse, double-click on the transaction.

   • Using the keyboard, highlight the transaction using ↑ or ↓ and press the Spacebar or select the Mark button.

8. When all desired transactions are added to the group, select the Done button.

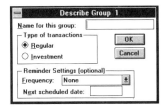

Figure 11.1   The Describe Group window.

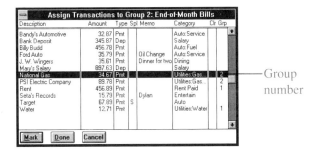

Figure 11.2   The Assign Transactions to Group window.

Using a Transaction Group

When you want to use a transaction group, you recall it in much the same way you recall a memorized transaction. Quicken automatically copies each memorized transaction in the group into the account register you specify. Follow these steps:

1. Pull down the Lists menu and select Transaction Group, or press Ctrl+J. Quicken displays the Transaction Group List window (see Figure 11.3).

2. Select the transaction group you want to recall:

   - Using the mouse, double-click on the selection.

   - Using the keyboard, highlight the transaction group using ↑ or ↓ and select the Use button. Quicken displays the Use Transaction Group window (see Figure 11.4).

3. From the Target account drop-down list, select the account to which you want to add the transactions.

4. Check to make sure the date shown in the Transaction date field is correct, and correct the entry if necessary.

5. Select OK to enter the group of transactions into the register. Quicken displays a message reminding you to check the transactions and make any necessary changes, such as dollar amounts.

Figure 11.3   The Transaction Group List window.

Figure 11.4   The Use Transaction Group window.

Using Quicken's Billminder

If you installed Billminder when you installed Quicken, you can use it to remind you when you have checks to print, when a transaction group is due to be entered into a register, or when it's time to make electronic payments. (Electronic payments are an advanced feature not discussed in this book.) If you want to change the Billminder settings, you can select Billminder from the Preferences menu and have Billminder remind you:

- When you first start your computer (Billminder).

- When you start Windows (Billminder).

- When you start Quicken for Windows (Reminder window).

Billminder Options   When you use the Preferences menu to set Billminder options, you can only set it to display its reminders at Quicken for Windows startup. To have Billminder remind you at boot or Windows startup, you must select the options during Quicken installation.

Follow these steps to turn on the Billminder and choose settings:

1. Pull down the Preferences menu and choose Billminder. Quicken displays the Billminder Settings window.

2. If the Turn on Billminder check box isn't checked, select it to turn it on.

3. If you want Billminder to remind you in advance of checks and transactions that are due, press Alt+I and enter the number of days in advance you wish to be notified.

4. If you want a reminder when you start Quicken for Windows, select the Reminder Messages on Startup check box.

5. Select OK.

Writing Checks

In this lesson, you'll learn how to use Quicken's check-writing feature to create and print checks and automatically enter transactions in the register.

When To Use the Write Checks Feature

If you plan to print checks using Quicken for Windows, or if you are using an electronic payment service such as CheckFree, you should use the *Write Checks* feature. When you print a check or make an electronic payment, Quicken automatically enters the transaction in the account register. To avoid double-entering transactions in your account register, you should not use Write Checks if you will be writing checks by hand and entering the transaction into the check register yourself.

Writing Checks

You can use Quicken's Write Checks feature for any account: checking, savings, or money market. Follow these steps to write a check:

1. Click on the Accts icon or press Ctrl+A. The Account List window appears.

2. Highlight the account you want to use and select the Use button.

3. Pull down the Activities menu and select Write Checks, or press Ctrl+W. Quicken displays the Write Checks window (see Figure 12.1).

    Click this icon to open the Write Checks window quickly.

4. Enter the following information:

   Pay to the Order of   Enter the payee name in this field.

   Date   (Optional) Enter a new date in this field, if necessary.

   $ Amount   Enter only the amount in this field. Don't type dollar signs or commas. Enter a decimal point and cents only if applicable. Press Tab after entering a dollar amount; Quicken automatically spells out the amount on the next line.

   Address   Enter an address (up to five lines) in this field if you are mailing the check in a window envelope. Press Enter at the end of each line.

   Category   Use this field to enter a category and, if applicable, a class, the same way you enter these items in the check register. Press Ctrl+C to display the category list, Ctrl+L to display the class list, or type the first few characters of the category name to have Quicken automatically insert the name.

Electronic Payment If you are paying bills electronically, select the Electronic Payment check box. (This box only appears when you set up a CheckFree account using the Activities menu. Note that electronic payment is an advanced feature not discussed in this book.)

5. If you want to split the transaction, select the Splits button and assign the split categories as you learned in Lesson 9.

6. When all entries are correct, select the Record button to save the transaction and record it in the account register.

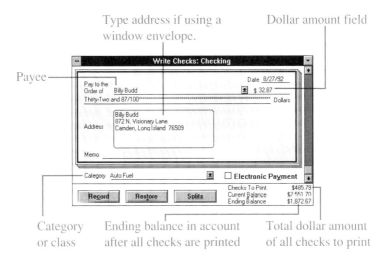

Figure 12.1 The Write Checks window.

Entering an Address If you are entering an address, Quicken can automatically enter the Payee name on any line of the address. Place the cursor where you want the name inserted and type ' or ". Quicken inserts the name and leaves the cursor at the end of the name.

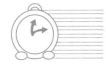

Once you save a check, Quicken automatically copies the transaction to the account register you are using. In the register, the check number field displays Print until the check is printed.

Reviewing and Editing Checks

When you write a check, Quicken automatically enters the transaction in the account register, but you still have time to review and, if necessary, edit the check. Before a check is printed, you can review and edit it in the check register or in the Write Checks window. After a check has been printed, you cannot edit it; you can only review the check in the check register. Use any of the following keys to move around in the Write Checks window:

Press:	To:
Ctrl+Home	Go to the first check.
Ctrl+End	Go to the last check.
Page Up	Scroll backward one check at a time.
Page Down	Scroll forward one check at a time.
Tab	Move forward from field to field.
Shift+Tab	Move backward from field to field.

To change an entry in a check, move to the field you want to change and retype the entry.

Finding a Check

When you have written several checks, you can quickly find a check in the Write Checks window using the Find command on the Edit menu, or by using the scroll bar. Refer to Lesson 8, where both of these methods are described for finding a transaction in a register. Use the same steps for finding a check in the window.

Voiding a Check

In certain cases, you might find it necessary to void a check. For instance:

- To stop payment on a check.

- To account for a lost check.

- To cancel a printed check that contained an error or didn't print correctly.

Voiding a check is the preferred method in these cases because the transaction can still be tracked. When you void a check, Quicken:

- Enters the word VOID before the Payee name on the check and in the check register.

- Deletes the amount of the transaction to adjust the register balance.

- Places an X in the Cleared column of the register so that the transaction does not affect the balance when you reconcile the account.

- If applicable, removes dollar amounts from the Splits window.

Use the following steps to void a check in the Write Checks window.

1. In the Write Checks window, select the check you want to void.

2. Pull down the Edit menu and select Void Transaction, or press Ctrl+V.

3. Select the Record button.

Deleting a Check

There may be times when you want to delete a check rather than void it. For example, if you inadvertently enter a check number that doesn't exist, there is no reason to keep a record of it by voiding it. You can delete it by doing the following:

1. In the Write Checks window, select the check you want to delete.

2. Pull down the Edit menu and select Delete Transaction, or press Ctrl+D. Quicken displays a message asking if you want to delete the transaction.

3. Select Yes to delete the check and the transaction.

Lesson 13
Printing Checks

In this lesson, you'll learn how to print checks using Quicken.

Purchasing Checks

To use Quicken for Windows' check-printing feature, you must use checks ordered from Intuit or another supplier of Quicken checks. Checks are available for the following types of printers:

- Continuous-feed printers

- Page-oriented printers (laser, inkjet, and tray-fed dot-matrix printers)

To find out about the various types of checks you can order and to print an order form, pull down the Help menu and select Order Supplies.

Setting Up Your Printer

Before you can print checks, you need to tell Quicken what kind of printer you are using. Follow these steps:

1. Pull down the File menu, select Printer Setup, and select Check Printer Setup. The Check Printer Setup dialog box appears (see Figure 13.1).

2. From the Printer drop-down list, select the printer you want to use to print checks.

3. (Optional) To override the auto-detect paper feed setting, pull down the Paper Feed drop-down list, and select Continuous or Page-oriented.

4. (Optional) To change the font used for printing the checks, select the Font button, make your selections, and select the OK button.

5. (Optional) To change any of the other printer settings (such as paper height and print quality), click on the Settings button, enter your changes, and click on OK.

6. Select OK to save the printer settings.

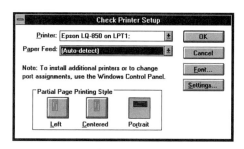

Figure 13.1 The Check Printer Setup dialog box.

Changing the Check Settings

Quicken lets you control the date format and various other settings that affect checks. To change these settings, pull down the Preferences menu and select Checks. The Check Settings dialog box appears, allowing you to:

- Change the format of the date.

- Add an extra message line to the check.

- Print categories on voucher checks.

- Display a warning if a check number is reused.

- Use the printing date as the check date.

Printer Settings   Quicken adjusts the printer settings shown in the printer Setup window based on the type of printer you select. Usually the settings are correct and do not require any changes.

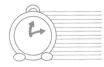

Positioning Checks and Printing a Sample Check

Before you print real checks, it's best to print sample checks until you're sure that your printer is set up correctly. Once you have the correct settings, you shouldn't have to change settings again unless you use a different type or style of check. Follow these steps to position and print sample checks.

1. Insert the checks the way you normally insert paper for your particular type of printer. (Use the sample checks that came with Quicken.)

2. Turn the printer on and make sure it is ready to print.

3. Pull down the File menu and select Print Checks. Quicken displays the Print Checks window as Figure 13.2 shows.

4. From the Check Style drop-down list, select the correct check style.

5. Select the Sample button, and select OK, if necessary. Quicken prints a sample check and then displays a dialog box asking if the check needs alignment.

6. If the print is aligned properly on the check, select OK or No to skip the alignment procedure.

   If the print is not aligned properly on the check:

   • If you are printing on a continuous-feed printer, go to the Position Number text box (see Figure 13.3), type the number that the POINTER LINE points to on the printed check, and select OK. Then, repeat step 5.

   • If you are using a laser or ink-jet printer, select Yes to display the Check Printer Alignment dialog box (see Figure 13.4). Move the mouse pointer to Payee, and drag it to where it appears on the printed check; then, click on OK. Repeat step 5.

7. When the sample check prints correctly, you are ready to print real checks.

Print checks
dialog box for
continuous-
feed printer

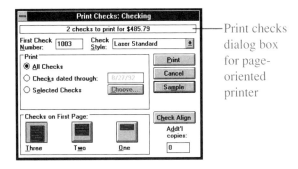

Print checks
dialog box
for page-
oriented
printer

Figure 13.2   The Print Checks window.

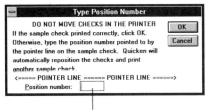

Type the number to which the POINTER
LINE points on the printed check.

Figure 13.3   The Type Position Number dialog box.

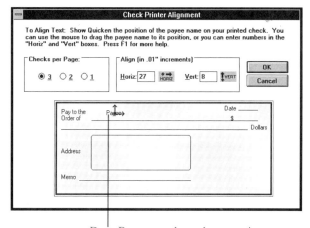

Drag Payee to where the payee's
name appears on the printed check.

Figure 13.4   The Check Printer Alignment dialog
box.

Printing Checks

To print checks, follow these steps:

1. Make sure that the checks are inserted correctly for your type of printer.

2. Make sure the printer is turned on and ready to print.

3. Pull down the File menu and select Print Checks. Quicken displays the Print Checks window.

4. If necessary, enter the number of the first check in the printer in the First Check Number field.

5. From the Check Style drop-down list, select the correct check style.

6. In the Print box, select one of the following settings:

   - All Checks prints all unprinted checks.

   - Checks Dated Through prints all checks through the specified date.

   - Selected Checks prints the checks you choose. Select the Choose button. To prevent a check from being printed, highlight it and press the Spacebar or select Mark. When a check is selected, the last column reads Print. Select OK to return to the Print Checks window.

7. If you are printing on a page-oriented printer, select Three, Two, or One in the Checks on First Page box.

8. Select the Print button. Quicken starts printing the checks.

   When finished, Quicken displays a dialog box asking if the checks printed correctly. If the checks look bad, select the appropriate option. You can adjust the alignment of the checks (assuming that is the problem) and reprint the checks as explained in the next section.

Stop Printing   If you need to stop printing for any reason, select the Cancel button in the Print Checks window. Your printer may continue to print for several seconds, but should stop after the printer memory is empty. If it doesn't stop printing after several seconds, turn the printer switch off.

Reprinting Checks

If necessary, you can reprint checks by performing the following steps:

1. Open the account register.

2. Select the transaction for the check you want to reprint, and type `Print` in the Num field.

3. Pull down the File menu, select Print Checks, and follow the steps described earlier in this lesson for printing checks.

Lesson 14

Reconciling an Account

In this lesson, you'll learn how to reconcile a Quicken checking account register against your statement from the bank.

Understanding Reconciliation

In Quicken, you'll need to *reconcile* several types of accounts, primarily checking and credit card accounts. This lesson uses the check register as an example because it is the most common type of account to reconcile. Once you learn the steps, you can apply them when reconciling other types of accounts.

Reconciling an Account   When you reconcile an account, you are checking to make sure that your records match the records kept by your bank. You are trying to see if your account has the same amount of money in it as *you think* it has in it.

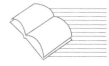

The basic steps for reconciling an account are:

1. Enter information from the bank statement, including the statement's balance and date.

2. Check off the transactions that have cleared the bank (that is, transactions that appear on the bank statement).

3. Compare the totals of cleared items between your register and the bank statement.

4. Make any necessary adjustments to balance the account.

Entering Information from Your Bank Statement

The first step in the reconciliation process is to enter information from your statement into your Quicken register.

1. Open the register for the account you want to reconcile.

2. Pull down the Activities menu and select Reconcile. Quicken displays the Reconcile Register with Bank Statement dialog box (see Figure 14.1).

 Click this icon to open the Reconcile Register with Bank Statement dialog box quickly.

3. Make sure the amount shown in the **B**ank Statement Opening Balance text box is the same as the amount shown under "beginning balance" or "previous balance" on the bank statement.

4. In the Bank Statement Ending Balance text box, enter the "ending balance" or "current balance" amount from the bank statement.

5. In the Service Charge text box, enter the total amount of service charges, if any, that you have not yet entered in your check register. In the Category box, you may categorize the service charges.

6. In the Interest Earned text box, enter the amount of interest, if any, shown on the bank statement. In the Category box, you may categorize the interest earned.

7. Select OK. Quicken automatically enters the service charges and interest earned into your check register and displays the Reconcile Bank Account window (see Figure 14.2).

Figure 14.1 The Reconcile Register with Bank Statement dialog box.

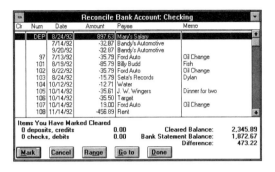

Figure 14.2 The Reconcile Bank Account window.

Marking Cleared Transactions

The next step in the reconciliation process is to mark all cleared transactions.

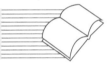

What Is a Cleared Transaction? A cleared transaction is one that the bank has processed and has noted on your bank statement.

The Reconcile Bank Account window, shown in Figure 14.2, contains a list of all uncleared transactions in your checking account. Follow these steps to mark cleared transactions:

1. Find each transaction in the Reconcile Bank Account window that is also listed on your bank statement. This includes checks written, deposits made, funds transferred, ATM withdrawals, ATM deposits, and any other transactions that affect the balance of the account.

2. Check to make sure each transaction amount matches the amount shown on the bank statement. If the amounts don't match, and if the error is yours,

- Click in the register's window or press Ctrl+R.

- Find the transaction and correct the error.

- Select the Record button.

- Return to the Reconcile window by clicking in it or selecting Reconcile from the Activities menu.

If you are sure that the bank made the error, contact the bank; don't enter a correction in your register.

3. In the Reconcile window, select a transaction by clicking once or highlighting it and selecting the Mark button. Quicken places a check mark in the Clr column. (It's a good idea to check off each transaction on the bank statement as you mark it in the Reconcile window.)

You can also mark or unmark a transaction by highlighting it and pressing the Spacebar.

Selecting a Range of Checks   When a range of checks has been cleared, you can select all of them at once by selecting the Range button and entering the first and last check numbers in the range. Quicken places a check mark in the Clr column for each transaction in the range.

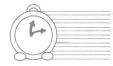

4. If the bank statement lists a transaction that is not shown in the Reconcile window, enter it now.

- Click in the register's window or press Ctrl+R.

- In the register, move to the first blank transaction (press Ctrl+N).

- Use the steps you learned in Lesson 7 to enter the transaction.

- Mark the transaction as cleared by entering an asterisk (*) in the C (Cleared) field in the register.

- Select the Record button.

5. Repeat step 4 for all transactions listed in the bank statement but not shown in the Reconcile Bank Account window.

As you use the preceding steps to mark transactions, Quicken continually increases the Cleared Balance shown in the lower right corner of the Reconcile window. With each cleared transaction you mark, you'll notice that the amount in the Difference field moves closer to zero.

Completing the Reconciliation

If the amount shown in the Difference field is zero, you have successfully balanced the account. (If the Difference amount is not zero, go to the next section, "Entering Adjustments.") Follow these steps to complete the reconciliation process.

1. In the Reconcile window, select Done. In the register, Quicken puts an X in the C (Cleared) column for each transaction you marked. Quicken displays a message asking whether you want to create a reconciliation report.

2. (Optional) To create a report, select Yes. Quicken displays the Reconciliation Report Setup dialog box.

3. Enter the appropriate information in the dialog box and select Print .

Entering Adjustments

After marking cleared transactions, correcting incorrect dollar amounts, and entering missing transactions, if the amount in the Difference field is not zero, the account is not balanced. You have two options to correct the problem:

- Have Quicken adjust the balance for you.

- Try to find the discrepancy in transactions between the check register and the bank statement.

When the difference is small, you may decide to have Quicken adjust the balance for you. Here's how.

1. In the Reconcile window, select Done .

2. If Quicken finds a discrepancy in the Opening Balance amount, you may have entered the wrong amount from the statement. You will be asked if you want Quicken to make that adjustment. Select Adjust Balance if you want Quicken to adjust for the discrepancy.

3. If the discrepancy is due to a transaction amount, you may have made an error when entering or making a transaction. Quicken tells you the amount and asks if you want the balance adjusted. Select Adjust Balance to have Quicken resolve the discrepancy.

If you decide the amount is too large to adjust and you want to find the discrepancy, use these guidelines:

- The Reconcile window shows the number of deposits and credits, and the number of checks and debits. Make sure these match the number shown on the bank statement. You may have forgotten to enter a transaction.

- The Reconcile window shows the total dollar amount for deposits (credits) and the total dollar amount for checks (debits). Make sure these match the dollar amounts shown on the bank statement. You may have entered an incorrect dollar amount.

Lesson 15

Working with Credit Accounts

In this lesson, you'll learn how to enter transactions in a credit account register.

Setting Up a Credit Account

Credit accounts can be for credit cards, like MasterCard, or for other types of credit accounts, as at your local business supply or office furniture store. If you pay the total balance at the end of each month, you probably don't need to set up a credit account unless you want to apply the charges to categories. You should set up an account for each credit account that you don't pay off in full each month. Setting up an account lets you track your charges and payments against the account, categorize the charges, and reconcile the statement at the end of each month.

To set up a credit account, follow these steps:

1. Pull down the Activities menu and select Create New Account. The Select Account Type dialog box appears.

2. Select Credit Card Account and select OK. Quicken displays the New Account Information dialog box (see Figure 15.1).

3. Enter a name for the account, such as Visa or Master-Card, in the Account Name box. The name can be up to 15 characters. (Don't use [ ] : or / in the name.)

4. In the Balance text box, enter the balance as of the current date. Be sure to enter the decimal point if the balance includes cents (for example, enter 986.42).

5. If necessary, tab to the as of text box and enter the date of the balance.

6. If this is an IntelliCharge account, select IntelliCharge to put an X in the check box.

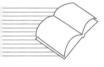

   What's IntelliCharge?   IntelliCharge is a special credit card you can get from Intuit. With IntelliCharge, you get your monthly statement on disk or via modem. For details, refer to your Quicken for Windows documentation.

7. (Optional) Enter a description for the account in the Description text box.

8. (Optional) Enter the credit limit in the Credit Limit text box.

9. Select OK. Quicken creates the new credit account and automatically opens the account register in a separate window.

Figure 15.1 The New Account Information dialog box.

Entering Transactions in the Credit Card Register

You can enter transactions all at once at the end of the month or, if you want to know the running balance, you can enter each transaction as it occurs. The following steps briefly review how to enter transactions in a register.

1. Open the Account List by pressing Ctrl+A or by clicking on the Accts icon.

2. Highlight the credit account you want to use and select the Use button (or just double-click on the account).

3. Move the cursor to the first blank transaction line by pressing Ctrl+N.

4. Enter a date in the M/D Year field.

5. Enter the name of the payee in the Payee field.

6. Enter an amount in the Charge or Payment field.

7. (Optional) Enter a memo in the Memo field.

8. (Optional) Enter a category in the Category field, or select the Splits button to split the transaction between multiple categories.

9. When all entries are correct, select the Record button.

Reconciling Your Credit Account and Paying Bills

Credit accounts are reconciled in much the same way as bank accounts: you enter information from the monthly statement into Quicken, mark all cleared transactions, and enter any missing transactions. Here's how:

1. Make sure the credit register is the active window.

2. Pull down the Activities menu and select Pay Credit Card Bill. Quicken displays the Credit Card Statement Information dialog box (see Figure 15.2).

3. In the Charges, Cash Advances text box, enter the total amount of the charges and advances shown on your statement.

4. In the Payments, Credits box, enter the total amount of payments and credits shown on the statement.

5. In the New Balance box, enter the amount shown on the statement.

6. In the Finance Charges box, enter finance interest charges, if any, as shown on the statement.

7. Select OK. Quicken displays the Pay Credit Card Bill window, shown in Figure 15.3.

8. Reconcile the statement the same way you reconcile your bank statement (refer to Lesson 14, if necessary):

   • Mark each cleared transaction.

   • Enter missing transactions.

   • Correct transaction amounts that were entered incorrectly.

9. Check to see that the amount shown in the Difference field is zero. If it is, select the Done button. If it is not, see the section "Entering Adjustments" in Lesson 14 to complete the reconciliation.

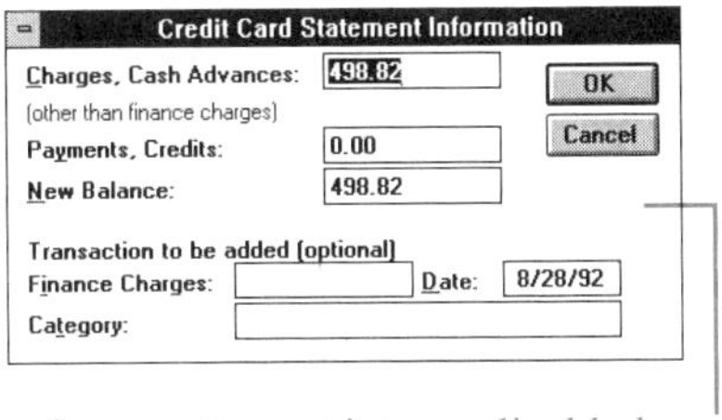

Enter information from statement into applicable boxes.

Figure 15.2   The Credit Card Statement Information dialog box.

Figure 15.3   The Pay Credit Card Bill window.

Paying Your Bill

Once your account is balanced, Quicken displays the Make Credit Card Payment dialog box shown in Figure 15.4. Follow these steps to pay the bill now, or select the Cancel button if you want to pay the bill later.

1. In the Bank Acct field, select the account from which you want to pay the bill.

2. In the Payment will be box, select:

   • Printed to have Quicken print the check.

   • Hand Written if you will write the check yourself.

   • Electronic if you use an electronic bill-paying service, such as CheckFree.

3. Complete the payment transaction as you normally would.

Figure 15.4 The Make Credit Card Payment dialog box.

Lesson 16

Working with Cash Accounts

In this lesson, you'll learn how to enter transactions in a cash account register.

Setting Up a Cash Account

A *cash account* in Quicken for Windows helps you keep track of transactions that are paid in cash rather than by check or with a credit card. In a business, a cash account is useful for tracking petty cash.

Setting up a cash account is similar to setting up a bank or credit account as you learned in Lessons 4 and 15. The basic steps are as follows:

1. Pull down the Activities menu and select Create New Account. Quicken displays the Select Account Type dialog box.

2. Select Cash Account. The New Account Information dialog box appears (see Figure 16.1).

3. Enter a name for the account in the Account Name text box.

107

4. In the Balance box, enter the current amount of cash.

5. If necessary, change the date in the as of text box.

6. (Optional) Enter a description for the account in the Description text box.

7. Select OK. Quicken creates the new account and opens the register in a new window.

Figure 16.1   The New Account Information dialog box.

Entering Transactions in the Cash Register

The cash register is identical to the check register except for the column headings. Instead of Num (check number), Payment and Deposit columns, the cash account contains Ref (reference), Spend, and Receive columns. You enter transactions in a cash register just as you do in the check register. Refer to Lesson 7 for detailed instructions.

Recording Funds Withdrawn from a Bank Account

When you withdraw funds from your checking or savings account to place in your cash account, you must enter a payment in the bank account and a receipt in the cash account. However, with Quicken, you enter the transaction in either account, and Quicken enters the corresponding transaction in the other account. Here's how:

1. Open the cash account register.

2. Enter the date of the transaction, tab to the Payee field, and type Cash.

3. Tab to the Receive field and enter the amount of money you want to withdraw from your bank account.

4. Tab to the Category field, and enter the name of the bank account from which you want to withdraw the money (for example, [Savings] or [Checking]).

5. Select the Record button. Quicken records the money received and adjusts the cash account balance accordingly. Quicken also enters a corresponding entry in the Payment field of the register from which you withdrew the money.

Either Account Will Do   Whenever you complete a transfer of funds between two accounts, you can perform the transfer from either account.

Updating a Cash Account

Because a cash account is not monitored by anyone such as a bank or credit card company, you don't reconcile the account against a statement, but it's a good idea to update the account periodically. It's easy for a cash account to get "out of balance" due to small errors or minor transactions that are not recorded. When you update the account,

Quicken records an adjustment entry to balance the account. Follow these steps to update the account:

1. Make the cash register the active window. (Select the account, if necessary.)

2. Pull down the Activities menu, select Update Balances, and then Update Cash Balance. Quicken displays the Update Account Balance dialog box (see Figure 16.2).

3. Enter the amount of cash currently on hand in the Update this account's balance to text box. Quicken compares the amount you enter to the amount shown in the register and creates an adjustment transaction for the difference.

4. (Optional) You can categorize the adjustment amount by entering a category in the Category for adjustment field.

5. (Optional) You can change the adjustment date Quicken enters in the Adjustment date text box by editing the entry.

6. Select OK. Quicken enters the adjustment transaction in the register.

Figure 16.2 The Update Account Balance dialog box.

Lesson 17

Working with Asset and Liability Accounts

In this lesson, you'll learn how to track the value of the items you own and the items you owe.

Using Asset and Liability Accounts

Assets and *liabilities* are two accounting terms that refer to what you own (assets), and what you owe (liabilities). Many people keep track of assets and liabilities to determine their *net worth*—what would be left if they sold their assets and paid off their liabilities. If you have a business, you may use asset and liability accounts to track depreciation of company equipment, or keep track of money owed to suppliers. If you own a home, you can use an asset account to keep track of home improvements.

Other Asset and Other Liability Accounts 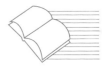 Quicken refers to an asset account as an *other asset account* because the primary asset account is a bank account. Quicken uses the same terminology to refer to liability accounts. In this lesson, the accounts you set up are referred to as simply *asset* and *liability* accounts.

111

Setting Up Asset and Liability Accounts

The steps used for setting up asset or liability accounts are similar to the steps used to set up any other type of account. Follow these steps:

1. Pull down the Activities menu and select Create New Account. Quicken displays the Select Account Type dialog box.

2. Select Asset Account or Liability Account and select OK. The New Account Information dialog box appears.

3. Enter a name for the account in the Account Name text box.

4. In the Balance text box, enter the current value.

5. If necessary, enter a date in the as of text box.

6. (Optional) Enter a description for the account in the Description text box.

7. Select OK. Quicken creates the new account and opens the register in a new window.

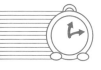

Setting Up Accounts for Individual Items or Groups You can set up asset or liability accounts for individual items or for groups. For example, if your business owns three pieces of equipment, you can set up an asset account for each, or you can set up a group account for all equipment. If you set up a group account, you can use classes to distinguish the three pieces of equipment.

Entering Transactions in Asset and Liability Accounts

Asset and Liability account registers are identical to the check register except for the column headings. Instead of Num (check number), Payment, and Deposit columns, the asset account contains Ref (reference), Decrease, and Increase columns (see Figure 17.1). The liability account contains Ref (reference), Increase, and Decrease columns (see Figure 17.2). You enter transactions in an asset or liability register just as you do in the check register. Use the Increase column in an asset account when the value of what you *own* increases. Use the Increase column in a liability account when the value of what you *owe* increases. Refer to Lesson 7 for detailed instructions on entering transactions.

Use this column when the value of what you own decreases.

Use this column when the value of what you own increases.

M/D Year	Ref	Payee / Memo	Category	Decrease	Clr	Increase	Balance
		Other Asset: Computer Stuff					
11/17 1992		Opening Balance	[Computer Stuff]			4,236 00	4,236 00
11/17 1992	*Ref*	*Payee* / *Memo*	*Category*	*Decrease*		*Increase*	

Record   Restore   Splits   1-Line   Ending Balance: 4,236.00

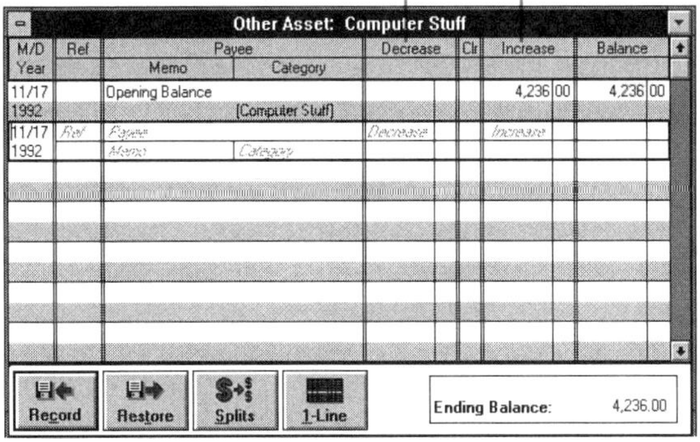

Figure 17.1   An Asset Account register.

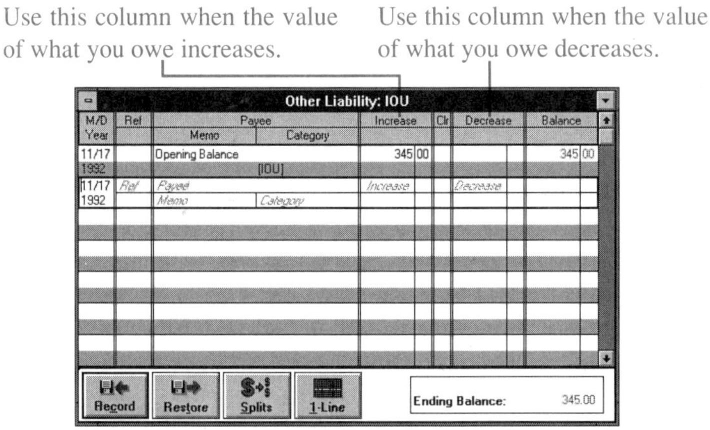

Use this column when the value of what you owe increases.   Use this column when the value of what you owe decreases.

Figure 17.2   A Liability Account register.

Updating Asset and Liability Accounts

Asset and liability accounts don't need to be reconciled, but from time to time you may want to update them. For example, if you own property for which the value has steadily risen from year to year, you would want to update your property asset account every year to reflect the current value. Follow these steps to update both asset and liability accounts:

1. Make the asset register or the liability register the active window.

2. Pull down the Activities menu, select Update Balances, and then select Update Cash Balance. Quicken displays the Update Account Balance dialog box shown in Figure 17.3.

3. Enter the current value of the asset or liability in the Update this account's balance to text box. Quicken compares the amount you enter to the amount shown in the register and creates an adjustment transaction for the difference.

4. (Optional) You can categorize the adjustment amount by entering a category in the Category for adjustment text box.

5. (Optional) You can change the adjustment date Quicken entered in the Adjustment date text box by editing the entry.

6. Select OK. Quicken enters the adjustment transaction in the register.

Figure 17.3 The Update Account Balance dialog box.

Lesson 18

Creating and Printing Standard Reports

In this lesson, you'll learn how to create standard Quicken reports and how to print them. .

Quicken's Standard Reports

By now, you've probably entered a great deal of information into Quicken to track your income and expense items, but to really manage your finances, you need to create reports. With reports, Quicken tallies up the transactions and puts the figures in a meaningful form. Quicken contains a variety of standard (preset) reports, which are listed by category in Table 18.1.

Table 18.1   Quicken's standard reports.

Category	Reports Available
Home	Cash Flow
	Monthly Budget
	Itemized Categories
	Net Worth
	Tax Summary
	Tax Schedule

Category	Reports Available
Business	PL (Profit/Loss) Statement
	Cash Flow
	A/P (Accounts Payable) by Vendor
	A/R (Accounts Receivable) by Customer
	Job/Project
	Payroll
	Balance Sheet
Investment	Portfolio Value
	Investment Performance
	Capital Gains
	Investment Income
	Investment Transactions

Note that investment reports are not discussed in this book. If you prefer to create custom reports, see Lesson 19.

Setting Report Preferences

You can change many of the default settings that Quicken uses for generating reports by selecting Reports from the Preferences pull-down menu. This displays the Report Settings dialog box (see Figure 18.1). Select the desired settings, and then select the OK button. For example, you can have the report include both the name and description of all accounts listed, and you can specify the range of dates that the report should cover.

Enter the default settings for your reports here.

Figure 18.1   The Report Settings dialog box.

Creating Standard Reports

It's not necessary to select an account before you create a report. Quicken draws information from whatever accounts are necessary to create the type of record you choose. To create a standard Quicken report, follow these steps:

1. Pull down the Reports menu, select Home or Business and select the type of report you want to create. Quicken displays a dialog box similar to the one Figure 18.2 shows. (The title of the dialog box varies depending on the type of report you choose.)

2. (Optional) Enter a title for the report in the Report title text box. If you don't enter a title, Quicken uses a standard title, such as "Cash Flow Report."

3. If the dialog box contains drop-down list boxes for a time period, enter a date in the Report from and to boxes, or pull down the list and select a date.

4. Select OK to create and display the report. A sample report is shown in Figure 18.3.

Enter the range of dates you want the report to cover.

Figure 18.2 The Create Cash Flow Report dialog box.

The Settings Button The Settings button (see Figure 18.2) lets you set custom options for a standard report without actually creating a custom report. To learn how to set these options, see "Selecting Special Options for Custom Reports" in Lesson 19.

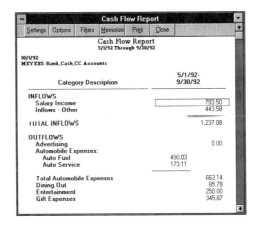

Figure 18.3 A sample Cash Flow Report.

Using QuickZoom to Investigate Transactions

If you see a total in a report that just doesn't look right, you can use the QuickZoom feature to view the transactions that contribute to that total. Here's how:

1. Move the mouse pointer over the item you want to investigate until the pointer turns into a magnifying glass.

2. Double-click on the item. Quicken displays the QuickZoom report listing the transactions that are related to the selected item (see Figure 18.4).

3. Double-click on a transaction in the list to view it in its register.

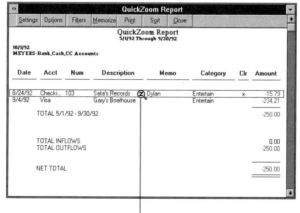

Double-click on a transaction to go to it in the register.

Figure 18.4   The QuickZoom Report window displays a list of transactions that contribute to an item on the report.

You can modify the transaction in the register, if desired. When you record the modified transaction, Quicken automatically updates the report. You can close or minimize the register and the QuickZoom report windows at any time using the same techniques you would use for closing any window.

Setting Up Your Printer for Reports and Graphs

Before you print a report (or a graph), you should check the printer setup to make sure the proper printer is selected and the printer settings are correct.

1. Pull down the File menu, select Printer Setup, and select Report/Graph Printer Setup. The Report and Graphs Printer Setup dialog box appears.

2. From the Printer drop-down list, select the printer you want to use to print reports.

3. (Optional) To override the auto-detect paper feed setting, pull down the Paper Feed drop-down list, and select Continuous or Page-oriented.

4. (Optional) To change the font used for printing the report heading, select the Head Font button, make your selections, and select the OK button.

5. (Optional) To change the font used for printing the body of the report, select the Body Font button, make your selections, and select the OK button.

6. (Optional) To change any of the other printer settings (such as paper height and print quality), click on the Settings button, enter your changes, and click on OK.

7. Select OK to save the printer settings.

Printing Reports

Once your printer is set up to print reports, the process of printing a report is simple. To print the active report, follow these steps:

1. Turn the printer on and check that it is ready to print.

2. Make the report window the active window.

3. Click on the Print button at the top of the report window, or press Ctrl+P, or select Print Report from the File menu. Quicken displays the Print Report dialog box (see Figure 18.5).

4. In the Print to box, select Printer.

Printing a Report to Disk   If you want to print your report to a file on disk rather than on paper, choose one of the Disk options. You can then open the file and use its data in another program, like a spreadsheet or tax program, for example.

5. If your printer is capable of printing in draft mode, you may select the Draft-mode printing check box.

6. If your printer is capable of printing graphics, you may select Use graphic line drawing to have the total lines printed solid rather than dashed.

7. Select the Print button. Quicken starts printing the report.

Figure 18.5 The Print Report dialog box.

Creating Customized Reports

In this lesson, you'll learn about Quicken for Windows' custom reports and how to create them.

Types of Custom Reports

In addition to the standard Quicken reports, you can create any of the following custom reports:

Transaction   A list of all transactions from the registers you select.

Summary   Totals for each category, class, payee, and account. No individual transactions are shown.

Budget   A comparison of actual income and spending to budgeted income and spending.

Account Balances   Shows how much money you have or owe in each account and shows the total amount you have or owe. This report essentially shows your net worth.

Creating a Custom Report

The steps for creating any of Quicken's custom reports are basically the same. When you choose a report type, Quicken displays a Create Report window similar to the one shown in Figure 19.1. Some options in this window vary depending on the type of report you are creating. The example in this section shows you how to create a Transaction report. Use the same basic steps to create other types of custom reports.

1. Pull down the Reports menu, select Custom, and select Transaction. Quicken displays the Create Transaction Report dialog box (see Figure 19.1).

2. (Optional) In the Report Title box, type a name for the report. If you don't enter a name, Quicken uses the name "Transaction Report."

3. In the Transactions From box, type a beginning date or select a date from the drop-down list. In the To box, type the ending date or select a date from the drop-down list.

4. In the Subtotal By box, select an option from the drop-down list, or use the default setting, "Don't Subtotal."

5. In the Accounts to Report on box, select one of the following options:

   Current The report contains transactions only from the active window.

   All Accounts The report contains all transactions from all accounts listed in chronological order.

   Selected Accounts When you choose OK to create the report, Quicken displays a Select Accounts to

Include dialog box. In the dialog box, all accounts are selected in the Include in Report column. To exclude an account, highlight it and select the Mark button. When you are finished excluding accounts, select OK. Quicken returns to the Create Transaction Report window.

6. Select OK. Quicken creates the report and displays it on the screen in a separate window.

Specify a date range.

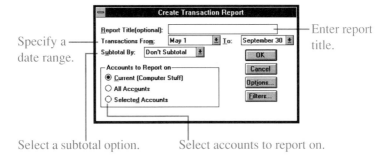

Enter report title.

Select a subtotal option.   Select accounts to report on.

Figure 19.1   The Create Transaction Report dialog box.

Recall from Lesson 18 that reports can't be saved, so if you want a permanent record of a custom report, be sure to print it.

Selecting Special Options for Custom Reports

Figure 19.1 shows the Options command button in the lower right corner. When you choose this button, Quicken displays the Report Options dialog box, shown in Figure 19.2. In this dialog box, you can select options that affect the way information is presented in a report. For example, you can choose to show split transactions or to sort transactions (for example, by date or check number). To set report options, follow these steps:

1. From the Create Report dialog box, select the Options button. Quicken displays the Report Options dialog box shown in Figure 19.2.

   If you've already created the report, you can display the Report Options dialog box by clicking on the Options button at the top of the report window or by pressing Alt+I.

2. In the Report Organization drop-down list, select Income and expense to organize the report by "Income," "Expenses," and "Transfers," or select Cash flow basis to organize the report by "Inflows" and "Outflows."

Options for Account Balances Reports   Note that when you create an Account Balances report, the options in the Report organization field are Net Worth format and Balance Sheet format.

3. Select an option from the Transfers drop-down list.

4. Select any of the following check boxes:

   Include Unrealized Gains   Report shows realized gains on paper only. (Use only for investment reports.)

   Show Totals Only   Display totals only; no transaction detail.

   Show Split Transaction Detail   Split transaction detail is shown in the report.

Show Cents When Displaying Amounts All dollar
amounts include cents.

5. Select an option for displaying memo and category
   information from the Memo/Category Display drop-
   down list.

6. Select an option for displaying subcategory information from the Subcategory Display drop-down list.

7. To sort transactions, select an option from the Sort
   Transactions By drop-down list.

8. When all settings are correct, select OK to return to the
   Create Transaction Report dialog box. To create the
   report, select OK.

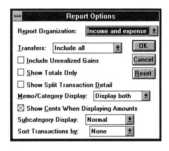

Figure 19.2   The Report Options dialog box.

Selecting Special Filters for Custom Reports

In addition to the Options command button, Figure 19.1
also shows a Filters command button. Select this button to
display the Filter Report Transactions dialog box, from
which you can restrict the transactions included in the

report. For example, you may want to view transactions for a specific payee. Use these steps to set filters:

Transaction Filter A filter allows you to specify the information you want included in the report. It filters out all other information.

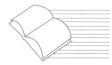

1. From the Create Report dialog box, select the Filters button. Quicken displays the Filter Report Transactions dialog box (see Figure 19.3).

   If you've already created the report, you can display the Filter Report Transactions dialog box by clicking on the Filters button at the top of the report window or by pressing Alt+T.

2. To display transactions for a specific payee, enter the payee name in the Payee Contains text box.

3. To display transactions that include a specific memo, enter the memo in the Memo Contains box.

4. To display transactions from a specific category, enter the category name in the Category Contains box.

5. To display transactions from a specific class, enter the class name in the Class Contains box.

6. Select any of the following check boxes:

   Select Categories to Include Displays a dialog box from which you can choose categories to include in the report.

   Select Classes to Include Displays a dialog box from which you can choose classes to include in the report.

Tax-Related Categories Only   Displays only those categories that are marked as tax-related.

7. Use the Transaction Amounts drop-down list to restrict the report to transactions of a specified dollar amount, and enter the dollar amount in the text box for The Amount .

8. Use the Transactions to Include drop-down list to restrict the type of transaction.

9. Under Cleared status , select either Blank , Newly Cleared(*) , or Reconciled(X) to specify whether you want to include only cleared transactions in the report.

10. When all settings are correct, select OK . Quicken returns to the Create Transaction Report dialog box. To create the report, select OK .

Figure 19.3   The Filter Report Transactions dialog box.

Lesson 20

Graphing with Quicken

In this lesson, you will learn how to get a clear picture of your finances with Quicken's graph feature.

The Graph feature is new to Quicken 2 for Windows. This feature allows you to graph your finances, view the graphs on-screen, and print the graphs for your own reference or to include in reports.

Types of Graphs

Quicken uses four types of graphs to display your data. The following list explains the various types:

- **Income and Expenses** Compares income to expenses to help you determine whether you are overspending or under earning. Displays a pie graph showing your top ten expenses to help you see your spending patterns. (See Figure 20.1.)

- **Budget Variance** Compares budgeted amounts to actual spending to help you determine whether you are sticking to your budget. To create a budget variance graph, you must first set up a budget, as explained in Lesson 21.

- **Net Worth** Uses account balances to compare what you own to what you owe, providing a clear picture of your net worth.

- **Investment** Uses data from your investment accounts to show how well one investment is doing compared to another, and to show the price history of an investment.

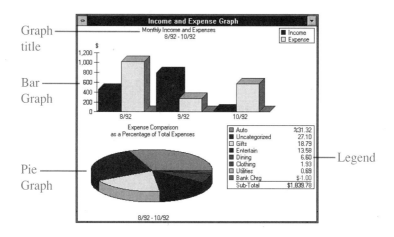

Graph title

Bar Graph

Pie Graph

Legend

Figure 20.1 An income and expense graph provides a breakdown of your expenses.

Creating a Graph

To create a graph, perform the following steps:

1. Pull down the Reports menu and select Graphs. The Graphs submenu appears, listing the various graph types.

Graphs Icon   To bypass the Reports menu, click on the Graphs icon in the iconbar. A dialog box appears, prompting you to select a graph type.

2. Select the type of graph you want to create. A Create Graph dialog box appears, as shown in Figure 20.2. The dialog box varies depending on the type of graph.

3. In the Analyze Months From and Through boxes, enter the first date and last date of the range of months you want the graph to cover.

   (To prevent the graph from being cluttered, make sure the graph covers 12 months or less.)

4. Click on any of the check box options to filter the accounts, categories, classes, or securities included in the graph. (For example, you can filter the accounts to show only your checking account.)

5. Select the Graph button. Quicken creates the graph and displays it on-screen.

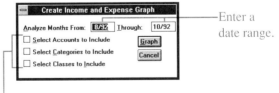

Enter a date range.

You can choose to exclude some accounts, categories, or classes.

Figure 20.2   The Create Income and Expense Graph dialog box.

Setting Graph Preferences

By default, Quicken displays graphs in color, prints them in black-and-white, displays two graphs inside each Graph window, and displays graphs in three dimensions. To change any of these settings, take the following steps:

1. Pull down the Preferences menu and select Graphs.

2. Select the option you want to change to put an X inside the check box.

3. Select the OK button.

Using QuickZoom to Investigate Items

When viewing a graph, you may want more detail concerning one of the items that appears. For example, if your auto expenses seem high, you may want to view a graph or a list of expenses. You can use the QuickZoom feature to view such detail:

1. Move the mouse pointer over the item you want to investigate until the pointer turns into a magnifying glass. (You can point to the item in the graph or in the legend.)

2. Double-click on the item. Quicken displays the QuickZoom Graph, showing a more detailed graph of the selected item (see Figure 20.3).

3. To view a detailed list of transactions, double-click on the portion of the detailed graph with transactions you want to view. A list of transactions appears.

Double-click here to display a transactions list.

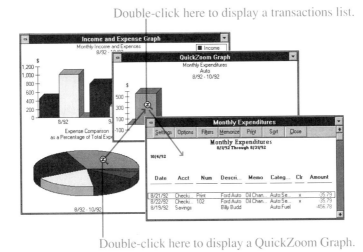

Double-click here to display a QuickZoom Graph.

Figure 20.3 Use the QuickZoom feature to view more details.

Printing Graphs

Before you print your graphs, make sure your printer is properly set up. If have not yet set up your printer, turn back to Lesson 18, and read the section called "Setting Up Your Printer for Reports and Graphs." Once your printer is set up, perform the following steps to print the graph that's displayed on-screen:

1. Turn the printer on and check that it is ready to print.

2. Make the graph window the active window.

3. Click on the Print button in the iconbar or select Print Graph from the File menu. Quicken starts printing the graph.

Lesson 21

Budgeting with Quicken

In this lesson, you'll learn how to use Quicken to set up a budget and print budget reports.

Understanding Budgets

Using a budget allows you to control your finances and set financial goals. By using a budget, you can see where your money is spent each month and determine where income is falling below expectations and where you need to cut back on expenses.

To compare actual income and expenses to budgeted income and expenses, Quicken uses categories. You set up the categories you want to use (or use Quicken's predefined categories), as explained in Lesson 5. You then specify the amount of money you plan to get or spend for each category, as explained in this lesson. Whenever you enter a transaction, you assign one or more categories to it, telling Quicken how much money you are making for each income category, and how much you are spending in each expense category. At any time, you can have Quicken generate a report or graph comparing the budgeted amounts to the actual amounts.

Setting Up Budget Amounts

Once you set up categories, you're ready to set up budget amounts. You can set up a budget in either of two ways. If you used categories to track expenses in the past (say for the last two months), you can have Quicken use this data to create a budget for you. Or, you can manually enter a budget amount for each category.

Letting Quicken Create the Budget

To have Quicken generate a budget for you using previously entered transactions, perform the following steps:

1. Pull down the Activities menu and select Set Up Budgets. Quicken displays the Set Up Budgets window (see Figure 21.1).

2. Select the Auto button in the Set Up Budgets window buttonbar. The Automatically Create Budget dialog box appears, as Figure 21.2 shows.

3. In the Apply and through text boxes, enter the range of dates from which you want Quicken to draw budget information. For example, if you have budget data only for August through October of 1992, enter 8/92 and 10/92.

4. To round the budget amounts to $1, $10, or $100, select an option from the Round values to nearest drop-down list.

5. Select one of the following options from the Fill Budget box:

With Monthly Detail Quicken will take the actual amounts from the months specified and insert them into the budget for only those months.

With Average for Period Quicken will take the average for each category, and copy the averages into the budget for all months.

6. Click on the OK button. Quicken fills in the requested budget information and returns you to the Set Up Budgets window.

7. Select the Close button in the buttonbar. A dialog box appears, asking if you want to save your changes.

8. Select Yes to save your budget information or No to exit without saving.

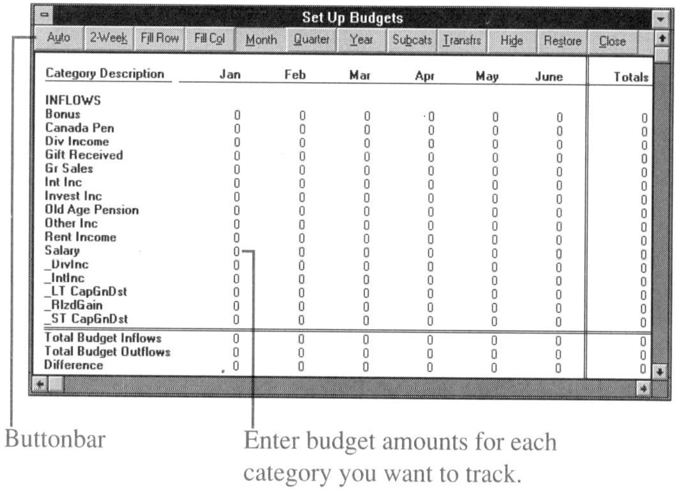

Buttonbar

Enter budget amounts for each category you want to track.

Figure 21.1 The Set Up Budgets window.

Enter the range of dates from which you want to extract data.

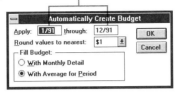

Figure 21.2 The Automatically Create Budget dialog box.

Restoring the Budget You can restore the budget to its original form by clicking on the Restore button. For example, if you start with a blank Set Up Budgets window, enter some budget amounts, and then decide that you want to start all over, select the Restore button.

Entering Budget Amounts Manually

Follow these steps to enter budget amounts for each category:

1. Pull down the Activities menu and select Set Up Budgets. Quicken displays the Set Up Budgets window you saw in Figure 21.1.

2. By default, Quicken sets up a monthly budget for 12 months. To set up a quarterly budget or a yearly budget, select the appropriate button from the Set Up Budgets window buttonbar: Quarter or Year.

3. To display subcategories, select the Subcats button; otherwise, Quicken will display only the main categories.

4. To display transfers in the budget, select the Transfrs button.

5. For each category, enter a monthly dollar amount. Use the Tab key or mouse to move to the next category or month, and use the following buttons at the top of the Set Up Budgets window to copy an amount to subsequent months:

   Fill Row   Highlight the amount you want to copy, and then select Fill Row to copy the amount for this category into all subsequent months.

   Fill Col   Enter the budget amounts for all categories in the current month. Then, select the Fill Col button to copy the budgeted amounts for all categories to the subsequent months in the year.

6. When amounts are entered for all categories, select the Close button in the buttonbar. A dialog box appears, asking if you want to save your changes.

7. Select Yes to save your budget information or No to exit without saving.

Biweekly Paychecks   If you get paid every two weeks, you know that two months out of the year you get three paychecks instead of two. You can have Quicken automatically keep track of this for you. Move the highlight to the category row for Salary, and then select the 2-Week button in the buttonbar. This opens a dialog box that allows you to enter the amount of the paycheck and the date on which you get paid.

Creating Budget Reports and Graphs

Once you've set up budget amounts and assigned categories to your various transactions, you can have Quicken generate budget reports and graphs. These reports and graphs compare actual income and expenses to planned income and expenses. For information about creating budget reports, refer to Lesson 19. For instructions on creating graphs, look to Lesson 20.

Using the Financial Planning Calculators

In this lesson, you will learn how to use Quicken's new financial planning calculators to help you take control of your financial future.

Quicken 2 for Windows offers the following four financial planning calculators to help you plan your finances and develop solid financial strategies:

- Loan Calculator

- Savings Calculator

- College Planning Calculator

- Retirement Calculator

The most useful feature of any of the financial calculators is that they allow you to play "what-if" with your finances. For example, what if I take out a 15-year mortgage rather than a 30-year mortgage; how much more will my monthly payments be, and how much will I save? What if I continue putting $100 in my retirement account; how much will I have saved when I reach the age of 65? What if I save a little more? With the financial calculators, you simply plug in various numbers and get immediate answers.

Using a Financial Planning Calculator

Although the options available in the financial planning calculators vary depending on the calculator, the general procedure for using any calculator is the same. Perform the following steps to use a calculator:

1. Pull down the Activities menu and select Financial Planners.

2. Select the calculator you want to use: Loan, Savings, College, or Retirement. Quicken displays a Calculator dialog box for the selected calculator (see Figure 22.1).

3. In the Calculate box, select the item you want Quicken to calculate. Quicken uses the data you enter in the other fields to calculate the selected value.

4. If the calculator window has a group of Inflation options, set the options as desired. For example, in the savings calculator, you can have Quicken adjust your contributions and the final balance for inflation to show you what your money is really worth.

5. Enter an amount in each text box in the Information box. When you enter a value and then move to the next text box, Quicken calculates the value for the item specified in the Calculated box.

6. (Optional) Select the Schedule button to view the payment schedule. Quicken displays the payment schedule. This will vary depending on the calculator you are using. Some calculators do not offer this option.

7. Select the OK or Close button to close the Schedule window.

143

8. Select the Close button when you are done.

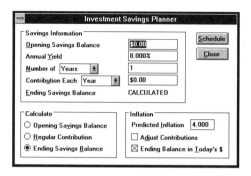

Figure 22.1   The Savings Calculator.

The Loan Calculator

With the loan calculator, you enter the principal (the amount you borrowed), the annual interest rate, the term (the number of years you have to pay off the loan), and the number of periods per year. The calculator determines the amount of the monthly payment, as shown in Figure 22.2. You can select the Schedule button to view a payment schedule that shows how much of each payment goes for principal and interest.

The Savings Calculator

The savings calculator (see Figure 22.1), can help you decide how much money you need to save in order to have a desired amount of money at the end of a specified time. The calculator can determine any of the following three variables, assuming you specify the other two variables:

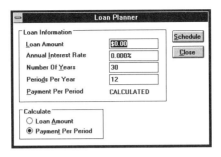

Figure 22.2 The Loan Calculator.

Opening Savings Balance   You specify the future value of the investment (how much you want the investment to be worth after the specified number of years), the amount of any additional contributions, the number of years, and the annual yield. Quicken determines how much you have to invest initially to meet your goal. You can also have Quicken account for the inflation rate.

Regular Contribution   You specify the present value (the initial investment), the future value, the number of years, and the annual yield. Quicken determines how much you have to contribute each year to meet your goal.

Ending Savings Balance   You specify the present value, the additional contributions, the number of years, and the annual yield. Quicken determines how much the investment will be worth at the end of the specified number of years.

Year/Quarter/Month/Week? With the Savings Planner, you can use the Number of and Contribution Each drop-down lists to calculate your savings by weeks, months, or quarters instead of by years. This is helpful if you have money automatically deducted from your paycheck and deposited into a special account.

The College Planning Calculator

How much money do you or your children need to go to college? How much do you need to set aside each year to meet your goal? To help you plan, Quicken offers the college planning calculator, shown in Figure 22.3.

You plug in the current tuition, the number of years until enrollment, the amount you have currently saved, and the annual yield, and Quicken determines how much additional money you have to set aside each year. Or, you can supply the annual payments, and have Quicken determine how much tuition you can afford. The calculator also adjusts for inflation.

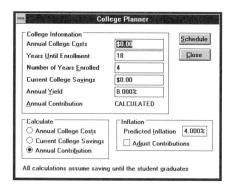

Figure 22.3 The College Planning calculator.

The Retirement Calculator

How much money should you be socking away for retirement? How much money will you have saved by the age of 65? How much can you expect to withdraw from your retirement account every year? And how much will those payments be worth when you are 65? The retirement calculator (see Figure 22.4) can tell you.

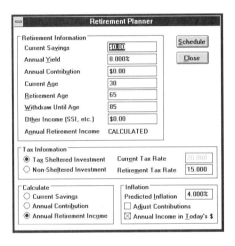

Figure 22.4 The Retirement Planning calculator.

Inflation   After you enter your current savings and your yearly contributions, the Annual Retirement Income figure might look rosy. But if you turn on the Annual Income in Today's $ option, you'll get to see the devastating effect that inflation has on your savings.

Lesson 23
Working with Quicken Files

In this lesson, you'll learn how to create and open new files and how to back up and restore important files.

Setting Up a New File

If you've been entering information into Quicken as you've worked through this book, the information has been stored in a file. Quicken automatically sets up a file (named QDATA) when you begin entering data. The file is actually four files (QDATA.QDI, QDATA.QDT, QDATA.QMT, and QDATA.QNX), which Quicken treats as a single file.

What Is a File? In Quicken, a *file* consists of all accounts that share the same categories, subcategories, classes, memorized transactions, reports, and so on. For example, when you enter personal financial data, Quicken creates a file that becomes the record of your home finances.

If you use Quicken for both home and business, you might want to set up separate files for each. To set up a new file, follow these steps:

148

1. Pull down the File menu and select New. Quicken displays the Creating New File dialog box.

2. Select the New File option and select the OK button. Quicken displays the Create Quicken File dialog box shown in Figure 23.1.

3. Enter a name for the file in the File Name text box.

4. Under Predefined Categories, select Home, Business, or both.

5. Quicken will create the file in the directory shown. If you want to create the file on a different drive or directory, select the drive from the Drives drop-down list, and select the directory from the Directories list.

6. When all settings are correct, select OK. The Select New Account dialog box appears. Refer to "Setting Up the First Time You Start Quicken" in Lesson 1 for instructions on how to proceed.

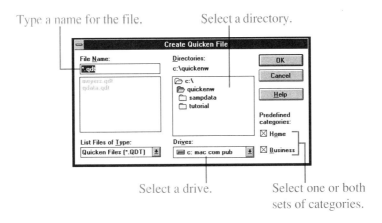

Figure 23.1 The Create Quicken File dialog box.

Opening a File

If you use only one file in Quicken, you never actually have to select a file to open; Quicken automatically opens the only file you have. If, however, you have created more than one Quicken file, you must select a file to open. Here's how:

1. Pull down the File menu and select Open, or press Ctrl+O. Quicken displays the Open Quicken File dialog box shown in Figure 23.2. Notice the current directory shown in the box. The files listed in the File Name list are the files in the current directory.

2. Select a file from the File Name list. If the file is not listed, it must be in a different drive or directory. Select the correct drive from the Drives drop-down list, and the correct directory from the Directories list; then select the file.

3. Select OK to open the file.

Select the file you want to open.

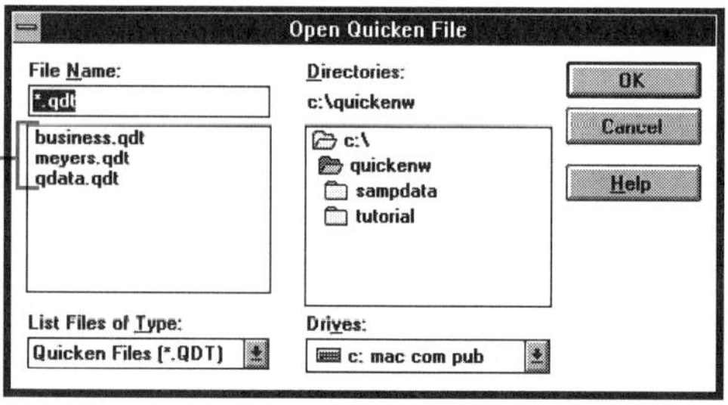

Figure 23.2   The Open Quicken File dialog box.

One File at a Time   If you already have a file open when you use the **O**pen command to open a different file, Quicken automatically closes the previous file.

Backing Up a File

Backing up a file is one of the most important things you can do to protect yourself from losing valuable data. You should back up all Quicken files regularly (daily, if you use Quicken on a daily basis, or perhaps weekly, if you use Quicken less frequently). You'll need a formatted floppy disk before you begin. Follow these steps:

1. Insert the formatted backup disk into floppy drive A or B.

2. Pull down the File menu and select Backup, or press Ctrl+B. Quicken displays the Select Backup Drive dialog box.

3. To back up the Quicken file that is currently open, select the Current File option. To back up a different file, choose the Select From List option.

4. Select the floppy drive from the Backup Drive drop-down list.

5. Select the OK button. If you chose the Select From List option, select the file you want to back up, and then select OK. Quicken begins backing up the file.

6. Quicken tells you when the backup is complete. Select OK, remove the disk, and store it in a safe place.

Restoring a File

You create backup files to protect your data in case you accidentally delete a file or one of your files gets corrupted. If this ever happens to you, you'll need to restore your Quicken files from your backup disk. Any transactions that you have entered since the last time you backed up your file will be lost. This is why it's important to back up a disk as frequently as you enter important data. To restore a file, follow these steps:

1. Pull down the File menu, select File Operations, and select Restore. Quicken displays the Select Drive to Restore From dialog box.

2. Insert a backup disk in the floppy drive, select a backup drive, then select OK. Quicken displays the Restore Quicken File dialog box.

3. In the File Name list, select the file to restore and select OK. Quicken begins restoring the file.

Index

C

printers, setting up, 86
   for reports and graphs, 121-122
printing
   Category & Transfer List, 37
   checks, 90-91
   graphs, 135
   reports, 122-123
pull-down menus, 13-15

Q

Qcards, instant help, 9-10
Qcards (Preferences menu)
   command, 10
QDATA file, 148
Quick Keys, 15-16
   Ctrl+A (Account List), 33
   Ctrl+B (Backup), 151
   Ctrl+C (Category & Transfer), 36
   Ctrl+D (Delete Transaction), 59, 84
   Ctrl+F (Find), 54
   Ctrl+J (Transaction Group), 73
   Ctrl+L (Class), 42
   Ctrl+M (Memorize Transaction), 66
   Ctrl+O (Open), 150
   Ctrl+T (Memorized Transaction), 68
   Ctrl+V (Void Transaction), 58, 84
   Ctrl+W (Write Checks), 80
   F1 (Help), 8
Quicken
   exiting, 10-11
   first time setup, 3-5
   starting, 1-2
Quicken for Windows program window elements, 6-7
Quicken Help (Help menu) command, 8
QuickFill, 64-66

QuickFill (Preferences menu) command, 65
QuickFill Preferences dialog box, 65-66
QuickZoom
   graphs, 134-135
   reports, 120-121
QuickZoom Report window, 120-121

R

Reconcile (Activities menu) command, 94
Reconcile Bank Account window, 95-96
Reconcile Register with Bank Statement dialog box, 94-96
reconciliation reports, creating, 98-99
reconciling accounts, 93-94
   adjusting balances, 99-100
   completing process, 98-99
   credit accounts, 104-105
   entering bank statement information into registers, 94-96
   marking cleared transactions, 96-98
registers, 30, 46-47
   asset, entering transactions, 113-114
   assigning categories or classes to transactions, 51-52
   cash, entering transactions, 108-109
   check, 47
   credit, entering transactions, 103-104
   entering bank statement information, 94-96
   liability, entering transactions, 113-114

159